The Literary Elephant

Books by JF Garrard

NON-FICTION
The Literary Elephant
How To Make a Munchkin

FICTION
International House of Vampires Series
Volume 1: The Undead Sorceress
Volume 2: Dark Evolution

Short Works
Designing Fate
Baby Shadows

The Literary Elephant:
The Beginner's Guide to Indie Publishing

JF Garrard

A Dark Helix Book

Published by Dark Helix Press Inc., darkhelixpress.com

Library and Archives Canada Cataloguing in Publication

Garrard, J. F., 1978-, author

The Literary Elephant : The Beginner's Guide To Indie
Publishing by JF Garrard, MBA.

Issued in print and electronic formats.
ISBN 978-0-9917425-4-7 (paperback).—
ISBN 978-0-9917425-8-5 (pdf)

1. Self-publishing--Handbooks, manuals, etc. I. Title.

Z285.5.G36 2015 070.5'93 C2015-905323-4
C2015-905324-2

DEDICATION

For Carolyn, one of the most optimistic doers I have ever known. There is one more angel in heaven, there is one more tear in my eye and we will always love you.

CONTENTS

PREFACE

While working on my first book, people kept asking me what it was like. "It was like giving birth," I replied. Since I have done both—given birth to a book and a live human being—I can say that they are comparable. Both require lots of planning and preparation before the big day. A lot of work is unseen and appears effortless to others. Both processes take a toll on your health. When I faced a brush with death during childbirth, I thought, *well, it's a good thing I have a legacy to leave behind: a baby and a book created from me to impart to the world. I hope both will do well in this world and make others happy.*

A book is never just printed pages filled with text. It is someone's story, their hopes and dreams. The moment you decide to indie publish, you have to become more businesslike in order to protect your heart from the onslaught of things that will happen, and to empower yourself to make business decisions not driven by emotion. You have to brace yourself for battle. In 2013 alone, 458,564 self-published titles were released in the US according to a ProQuest survey. This number doesn't count other countries such as the UK, which also publish many indie books.

As the availability of indie books rise, there is also a shift in the type of authors releasing them. People who publish quickly, pay no attention to detail, don't invest in proper editing, and generally do a crappy job in the production steps are finding it harder and harder to sell books. Readers are accepting indie publishing, but only supporting well made, quality products. Even if a book is free, the reader is still investing time in reading it and their time should be respected. Authors who create an excellent book by investing in editing, cover art, formatting, and design will build their very important reputation as good writers.

This is your book, your baby. All I can say is keep your mind open to new ideas and work hard, play hard. Success will come eventually, so do enjoy your indie publishing journey along with all the crazy adventures it will bring.

Your fellow indie author friend,

Jeannie Fong Garrard

August 2015

THE DIFFERENT PATHS OF PUBLISHING

---

*"If you find a path with no obstacles,
it probably doesn't lead anywhere."*

-Frank A. Clark

What Are the Paths Of Publishing?

As I write these words, shudders are still going through authors living in Canada after the Penguin Random House merger. It has been declared that unless a book can potentially reap over $100,000 in profit, it will not be picked up by the publisher. Selling books is a difficult business these days as books are competing with other forms of entertainment such as video games, television shows, and internet content. Not to mention that any profit (after editing, formatting, cover design, and marketing expenses) from book sales is split between the author, literary agent, publisher, and distributor. Overall, the message is that submitting a manuscript to a large traditional publishing company will usually result in the book not getting published. Typically, even when published, the writer will get the smallest cut of profit—normally something like 10% compared to the 70% publishers take. No wonder writers are often solemn people!

In this day and age, writers are lucky because there is more than one path to choose from. Indie (short for independent) or self-publishing has always existed for writers who had the financial means to go to the local print shop and create copies of their book for sale to the public. They would invest in typesetting and print runs of large orders—the larger the order, the more they would save on costs—and store everything in the basement, often for years on end because this path also means they are exclusively responsible for marketing! With the dawn of the internet and electronic books, authors can now upload their book and make it available to the world in mere minutes. Print on demand (POD) publishing replaces the print run bulk ordering technique and means that authors don't have to store inventory anymore. Books are not printed until a customer orders them. Technology has given more writers a more cost effective method for sharing their creations without the need to involve a publisher, or share their profits to as many parties.

When a reader picks up a book, it is usually because they really want to read the content by an author they respect. They don't really care about who published it or how it got into the book store or online retailer. What matters to them is that it is available for purchase in the form they prefer (eBook, hardback, paperback, audio), tells a great story, is legible, and professionally edited. Of course, making a book available for purchase is not a simple matter as there are many steps involved from draft manuscript to finished book. Regardless of any publishing path, there will be obstacles and the end goal is to make the book available to its readers.

Currently, a writer can choose from three publishing

paths, which includes:

1) traditional publishing

2) vanity press publishing

3) indie/self-publishing

We will go into each type of publishing in a bit more detail as a writer can consider one or more options for their works. Even if you decide to indie/self-publish, you can always submit another piece of work to traditional publishers at the same time.

A writer who publishes via traditional and indie methods is called a hybrid author. This will most likely become the trend for publishing as a writing career can be very long and by participating in both paths, the publishers have lower risks and writers can potentially earn more for themselves. The threat to the profits of a traditional publisher is not a new indie author, but a well-established hybrid author who already has a massive audience base.

Traditional Publishing

This is the path in which a writer finishes a piece of work and an agent helps them sell it to a publisher. The publisher provides the writer an advance payment under a contract giving them the right to distribute the work. A deal is worked out in regards to how the writer, agent, and publisher split future earnings, or royalties. The publisher then bears the responsibility for getting the product to market by providing staff for editing, cover design, art, and marketing. Since the publisher takes on the largest financial risk with each project out of all parties, they reap the most rewards as well. If the book sells really well and the royalties end up exceeding the advance, the author will get more checks. But that rarely happens.

Daniel Menaker, former head of Random House, wrote

in an article for Barnes & Noble's Review that "publishing is essentially a casino…three out of four fail to earn back their advances. Or four out of five or six out of seven, depending on what source you consult. And depending on what kind of accounting shell game is being played in the back office." Author Tara K Harper states on her website that only 3 out of every 10,000 manuscripts submitted to publishers are actually published. It's the one big winner that brings huge profits to the publisher. So it should not be a surprise that publishers are very picky about what projects they choose to take on. Regardless of risks, according to the International Publishing Association, 2013 publisher net revenue in the US totaled 19.56 billion €, 4.66 billion € in the UK, and 1.5 billion € in Canada.

Large publishers usually do not want writers to send in unsolicited manuscripts because it takes a lot of time to sort through mountains of correspondence. If you want to go this route, you will need to find an agent. A literary agent is similar to a Hollywood acting agent, but instead of signing an actor, a literary agent signs authors. They will help you sell your manuscript to a publisher and will receive a cut in return. If a royalty is earned on a book, typically the publisher takes 70%, the agent 20%, and the writer gets 10%. Usually, the writer's 10% is the advance received from the publisher. In recent years, instead of selling manuscripts to publishers, some agents are becoming consultants for self-publishing. They are not publishers, but rather they take a fee for guiding authors on how to self-publish while attempting to sell the sub rights, which includes foreign, audio, film, TV, and performance.

To find an agent, you will need to write a query letter and include part of your manuscript so they can analyze your style and determine if you are a good fit for them. If they feel like they can sell your work, they will take you on. Agents may specialize in different categories, such as young adult, romance, paranormal fiction, or nonfiction. If you are going to write to an agent, be sure to look up their profile and their submission guidelines.

Be aware that you may not get many, or any, responses from agents. According to Kristin Nelson, a staff member of Nelson Literary Agency, she received over 35,000 submissions, read 856 sample pages, read 45 full manuscripts, and only signed one new client in 2014. This is difficult news to digest. She only signed 1 out of 35,000 people to represent!

Here are a few websites where you can research literary agents. They also have resources for writers going through the query process:

agentquery.com
querytracker.net
writersmarket.com
publishersmarketplace.com

You may have read in the news about the success of books such as *Wool* or *Fifty Shades of Grey*. These books were self-published by the author and after gaining a mass audience, traditional publishers negotiated for the rights to them. It is less of a risk for the large publisher to purchase these manuscripts since the groundwork was already done by the author. They knew the book could be sold to certain audiences. This may happen more and more in the future as publishers can sign on authors who already have loyal readers following them and have proof of book sales.

Remember, creating a book is not just simply writing the manuscript. After writing, many steps need to happen before the book can be sold to a reader: in-depth editing, copy editing, proofreading, formatting, cover creation, printing, proper paperwork registration (ISBN, copyright, tax forms), and distribution. After these production steps, ongoing marketing has to happen in order to drives sales to pay for all the expenses that have already occurred.

The key difference between traditional publishing and indie publishing is that the publisher pays for all the steps required to publish and market a book. They invest their time, staff, and money, and use their established media contacts for marketing. An indie author has to hire people to help them package their book or use a lot of their own time. The breakdown for profit is a bit more lucrative with indie publishing as the author can receive up to 70% in royalties. However, an indie author will most likely not have the same marketing budget as a large publisher and will not sell as many books in comparison.

Regardless, a traditional publisher and indie author will have to go through the same steps of creating a book as mentioned before, but the difference is really in who gets to pay the bill and reap the profits. For the traditional publisher, standards are very high because they are competing with another publisher who has the same giant budget and army of staff that can create a great product for the reader. An indie author will have to hire professional freelance staff to help with book creation in order to achieve the same standards.

The trends I have mentioned about traditional publishers are specific to large publishing houses. Small presses are a different animal as they are smaller, independent companies with limited resources and are an alternative to the giant conglomerates. They have less bureaucracy and profit may not be their only or biggest motivation since they don't have shareholders to answer to. Small presses are easier for an author to approach directly with submissions and they can take on new authors deemed too risky by the larger publishers. Agents are not interested in them as they don't usually have the funds for book advances or commissions. Generally, a small press won't offer an advance to the author, but may give a higher royalty rate instead. Be wary if the small press starts asking you for money to cover costs as it may be a vanity press in disguise, something we will discuss next.

Before submitting to a small press, you may want to research their history to ensure that the company is stable because many go bankrupt even before publishing any books due to the high cost of running a business. Try to make sure the staff is competent before handing over your manuscript to avoid problems like schedule delays, terrible contracts, no marketing or distribution, and unpaid royalties. Ask questions about what they have done for other authors and see if they have a large reach by searching for some released titles. Look at their website to see if it's nicely done—this attests to their online and marketing skills.

Vanity Press Publishing

Vanity presses are publishers you can hire to publish your book for you. For some reason, people often get mixed up and think that vanity press publishing and indie publishing are the same thing. It is not, and there are huge differences.

Think of publishing your book as building a house. Do you want to hire a general contractor who will make all the decisions for you (flooring types and colors, wall colors, cabinetry styles, countertops, floor plan, number of rooms) and expect you to just pay whatever bill they hand you? Or do you want to build the house yourself by hiring a team of contractors who build to your style and design choices? A vanity press is a general contractor who has their own team and you may never meet any of the team members. If you build your own house, you can pick the contractors to suit your own needs, as well as build relationships with each service provider. Overall, you maintain control over the project if you are indie publishing. However, as one of my friends pointed out, she didn't have time to find people to work with, so hiring a vanity press was suitable for her needs.

Although traditional publishers have publicly denounced vanity press books as low quality, the truth is, most of them are owned by large traditional publishers. Over time, publishers realized that some authors didn't want to do all the indie publishing steps themselves and would rather pay to get all the work done and over with. So the publishers bought or created vanity presses (using different company names so as not to sour their main brand) and for a few hundred to thousands of dollars, someone can get their book published with minimal work.

A typical vanity press publishing package would include some copy editing, book cover creation, a few paperback copies, and perhaps include some retail book store shelf space. They also distribute to retailers on your behalf and take a cut of the royalties. Every month, you are supposed to receive a report of book sales and calculated royalty amounts. This is very different from indie publishing where you would have a direct account with the distributor to view sales numbers instead of relying on someone else giving you a report.

One of my author friends bought a vanity package which gave her only copy editing, a dozen paperback copies, and one book shelf space for one bookstore in Canada. The cost was about two thousand dollars. She thought it was worth it because she didn't have to do much work to get her book published. When I questioned why only copy editing was included and not in-depth, she said that her writing was so good she didn't need to pay for in-depth editing. She did complain that she had to do her own cover and the press release written for her book was awful. Her manuscript was returned as a PDF file and she had to pay a fee to correct each mistake. There were also monthly phone calls presenting new marketing tactics such as subscribing to indefinite plans for a few hundred dollars a month so the company would help negotiate a movie contract for the book. She also didn't know how many copies she sold every month as the reports were often late, as were the royalty payments. However, regardless of all this, she said she would most likely publish another book with the same vanity publisher as she didn't think there was a better way. Indie publishing was too much work for her and she was unwilling to go that route.

If you don't have much time or energy and you still want to choose to publish via a vanity press, I would recommend doing some research before forking over any of your hard earned money. Be very weary before signing anything as you may be signing away the rights to your book while paying for services. Read the contract very carefully and don't be afraid to ask questions.

Here are a few suggested questions you could ask:

- Do I keep the rights to my manuscript?

- What kind of editing is in this package?

- How does the editing process work?

- How much do edits to spelling mistakes in the manuscript cost after the process?

- Where are the books distributed?

- Does the package include a cover design or do you have to make one?

- How does the royalty distribution system work?

- What kind of paperwork will be provided for taxes?

Again, even if you go down the vanity press route, you can still choose to send manuscripts to traditional publishers or indie publish at a later date.

Indie or Self-Publishing

Out of all the options of publishing, indie publishing offers the most control and highest royalty percentages. With traditional publishing, after the author sells their manuscript, it becomes the publisher's project, and so all decisions will be made by the publisher from cover art to book launches. It doesn't matter if the author doesn't like the book cover because the marketing department is in charge of this. For vanity press publishing, the author has more say since they hired a company to help them finish their book, in theory. However, the author doesn't have control over the team hired for all the steps of publishing and distribution and will not have direct access to any sale records. If any mistakes are made along the way (typos in manuscript) or if the author changes their mind about the cover, the author will have to pay for each change. Additionally, an internet search of any vanity press name with the word complaints behind it will show that there are a lot of problems ranging from poor workmanship in editing steps to being charged for every little detail the author wants to change in any aspect of production.

For indie publishing, as compared to building a house before, you will pick and hire each service provider. Will it take more time than the other options? It depends. For traditional publishing, you may wait for months or years before the book comes onto the market as it takes time to make a deal, sign an agreement, and for the publisher to turn your manuscript into a book. Vanity presses admittedly could churn out a book the quickest, however, the author will still need to spend time double checking and possibly paying a bit more to ensure that a quality product gets released to market. Since you have more say in indie publishing, how fast or slow you put out a book depends on you and your efforts.

Before we go into more details about the steps of indie publishing, please take one piece of advice: DO NOT

QUIT YOUR DAY JOB! The latest Digital Book World's author survey conducted in 2014 concluded that on average, one third of authors earned about $1–$499 USD annually. This survey sampled about 2000 authors in which half self-published. There were of course outliers with huge incomes over $100K USD who are superstars. Overall, half of the writers surveyed, both traditional and self-published, earned $1,000–$2,999 USD or less. The lesson here is that if you like eating, don't rely on your writing income to feed yourself!

Becoming a successful self-published indie author is about one in a million according to a recent Forbes magazine article. Some authors are lucky and become the role models of the self-publishing world, like Amanda Hocking. Indie publishing is truly an act of love as breaking even may never happen or may take a long, long time. According to statistics gathered by Digital Book World and Writer's Digest author surveys for a 2015 report, 60% of indie authors sold fewer than 500 books. Other indie authors sell so well that publishers decide to make offers to invest in them. No matter if the book is published traditionally or self-published, the average book will sell about 250 copies to 2000 over its lifetime.

If you want to sell books, you will have to think a bit differently from when you were writing. From the moment you decide to indie publish, you must think of yourself as becoming an entrepreneur with a small business that involves selling books. It's a business because you will be investing time, money, and effort into making a high quality product. You will also want to break even or earn some profit. Regardless, your book is not just a great piece of creative writing; it's a product needing to be marketed to potential customers. Remember, your book will be competing with other indie books and traditional books for the same readers!

Indie publishing does not mean amateur publishing.

Because it is very easy to self-publish online, there is no gate keeper, or quality control. Some authors publish very quickly by releasing a book with no editing, terrible cover, and so on, just generally making it a poor product. This unfortunately causes some readers to recoil in horror after paying for such a product and swear off indie books forever. The market will only want to pay for a book with standards comparable to traditional publishers.

In the long run, if indie books are to be respected as much as traditionally published books, authors need to step up and invest in their work by ensuring quality manuscripts are sent to market. According to the Huffington Post, indie publishers made up 30% of the eBook industry while traditional publishers held 70% in 2013. As well, the New York Times bestseller lists now combine print and eBook titles, and indie authors are already appearing on this list. Self-published books appear on Amazon best seller lists regularly.

As you learn more about indie publishing, remember there is no shame in admitting you can't do everything yourself. You will learn over time what your strengths and weaknesses are. Even if try to do everything and not pay anyone else for help, don't forget that your time is worth something. Time is a precious commodity and should not be wasted. If you start dreading a certain task because it takes too long or the learning curve is too high, perhaps it's worth paying someone who can do a much better job for a small fee, freeing your time for something else that you enjoy. One area you cannot do on your own is editing because you are too close to the material—bear in mind, all the best writers in the world have an editor!

Competition is rampant within indie publishing and according to Bowker, the number of self-published books annually continues to increase. This number is up 17% over 2012 and 437% over 2008 numbers. It is expected that the number of titles will increase even more.

As more and more self-published books come out on the market, the only way to compete is to make sure your book is really, really good and professionally packaged. How do you do that? Well, by thinking, planning, and looking for the best team possible as I'll illustrate in the upcoming chapters.

2

POLISHING THE MANUSCRIPT

"So the writer who breeds more words than he needs, is making a chore for the reader who reads."

— *Dr. Seuss*

Words are the most important part of a book as they are the communication mechanism for your story to come to life in someone else's mind. Writing is the construction of complex creative and technical elements, which when done properly to the finest details triggers the reader's mind to see and feel and hear what you've created beyond the page in front of them. Often it's described as seeing a movie in the mind or imagining the characters, places, and actions as if they were playing out on a private movie screen. The writing is interpreted by the reader's conscious and subconscious, and if the words don't flow well and inspire the reading experience they expected, or better, they may set your book down and have only negative things to say about it. They would probably be quite annoyed too, for having invested time and money into such a book.

I have met more than one self-published author who thought their raw work good enough for the world and believed they didn't need to waste any time or money on an editor. It should not be a surprise that these people are not best sellers and have done so-so in the market (sold more than one, less than one hundred). If not already, more than likely there will be, reviews by the court of readers leaving judgments on the sale pages of these books, such as "poor editing/proofreading" and "needs editing/proofreading," signaling other buyers not to waste their time.

The editors I have used are all published authors, and they employ editors for their books. If a seasoned editor is unwilling to rely solely on their expertise and experience in the business of their published works, this tells me there must be a very good reason for always having a pair of expert, fresh eyes to ensure words accomplish what they were meant to.

Admittedly, this will be the most time consuming and perhaps expensive service you will require to prepare your book for publishing, but it is also the most essential to creating a quality product. If you know someone who is an editor, publishes their own books, and willing to trade editing for editing instead of cash, this mutually beneficial scenario can help you save money. Beware of trading with authors who are not experienced editors, however, as authors tend to be more influenced by creative factors and less skilled with following the appropriate style guide than a seasoned editing professional would be.

Why Hire An Editor?

Perhaps you are still not certain why an editor is required so here are a few reasons:

Reason #1 – Leveling the Playing Field

Realizing your book will be compared to books released by other publishers, big and small, with variety in the level of quality workmanship invested in each product, consider:

Why would someone want to buy your unedited book when they can easily buy from an author who worked with a good editor?

Traditional publishers employ or contract with experienced, cream of the crop editors to polish their manuscripts. Indie and self-published authors have access to an enormous pool of freelance professionals, including some with traditional publishing experience on their resumes. Seeking the right editor for your project can make all the difference, and you do have access to the same quality workmanship traditional publishers use.

Remember that your book has to be comparable to those from the big name authors and any lesser known author who has invested deeply in editing workmanship if you want to compete.

Reason #2 - Building Credibility as an Author

You have invested a lot of time, money, and effort into creating your book. Why throw this all away? Whether your goal is to eventually get picked up by a publishing house for a lucrative deal or sell books as a hobby, you want and need a good reputation behind your efforts to achieve success. Authors are known for their words and if your words sound amateurish, no one will ever take you seriously as a professional writer. Enough said.

Reason #3 - Improving Your Craft

Writing is a continuous and repetitive journey of write, edit, package, publish, market, and begin again. You need more than one product to build a reputation. Just like anything else, there is always room for improvement and professionals know their success grows as they learn and grow in their career path. Working with an editor affords a great opportunity to learn more about writing. An experienced editor who encourages questions and provides a nurturing work relationship is worth their weight in gold. The knowledge they share during the process would take you years to learn by yourself, not only for the style guide technicals, but also for marketing angles you may not have even thought about.

It was during the editing process for my first novel, *The Undead Sorceress*, when I realized I had included elements of cultural context into the book that only a small part of my market would immediately recognize and understand without realizing it. My editor is from the US and I was caught off guard by her question about "red pockets" mentioned in one chapter. They are red envelopes filled with cash and given out during special occasions in Chinese and some Asian cultures. My previous amateur editors (my husband and a friend) had received red pockets in the past, so they didn't question seeing them mentioned. In the final version of the manuscript, I wove explanation of the red pockets into the dialogue leading to clarity and a higher likelihood that more readers would relate and understand the Chinese/Asian characters overall.

Reason #4 - Respecting the Reader

Have you ever heard customers complain at the return desk of a department store? Or have you read bad product reviews online? Have you complained in either of those situations about a product you were unhappy with?

You do not want to piss off your readers; they are your friends and allies in marketing. In this age of social media, there is hell to pay if someone purchases your book and ends up feeling like they have been bamboozled. It doesn't matter if they got your eBook for free during a promotion, either. They invested their time into reading your book, and their time is valuable just like yours is. They could have been eating cupcakes or doing something else!

Reason #5 - Copy Blindness

This is the effect of an author creating and reading a manuscript so many times that they are not capable of seeing mistakes any more. This happens because the author knows more about the story than is on the page. There could be an obvious error in front of your face, but you won't see it. And because you created it, you will always see what you meant, not what you wrote. Understand that copy blindness is real and the cure for this is to find another set of eyes. Sometimes I also think the word processing program I use for typing my manuscript is possessed and changes the words on me. Words I intend to type seem to be magically replaced by ones spelled in a similar manner but with a different meaning.

The Different Types of Editors

There are different types of editing. The three types of editing include in-depth editing, copy-editing, and proofreading.

In-Depth Editing

The main focus of in-depth editing is to improve the story and develop its organization and structure. Big picture changes will be made during this phase to ensure the story being told makes sense and captures the reader's attention. This should always be done before copy-editing and proofreading. In-depth editing is often broken down into various levels so the editor reviews the material multiple times to be as thorough as is humanly possible. Since it consumes the most time and brain power due to detailed analysis of the manuscript, it will also cost more compared to the other types of editing. Discussion and sampling of your material allows the editor to help you determine at which level your manuscript should enter the editing process.

Developmental/Project editing and Substantives or Structural editing are two common levels of in-depth editing when divided into manageable portions. Some of what they look at:

- story organization, structure, pacing, and flow
- plot holes
- Point of View (POV) stability/accuracy
- character flaws and development
- dialogue suited to each character
- overall clarity and content
- logical presentation
- smoothing out awkward phrasing, conflicting statements, and irrelevant material
- intensifying beginning and ending to help satisfy readers
- problem/conflict solution is evident, believable, and relatable

Copy-Editing

Copy-editing looks at the mechanics of how the story is told. The editor's technique for focusing in this level of editing differs from the in-depth levels. Some of the aspects they check are:

- grammar, proper tense, and tone
- incorrect word use
- consistency of mechanics, facts, and spelling of author's fiction words and acronyms
- adherence to rules for capitalization, numbers,

italics, and punctuation

- clarity at the line and word level

Proofreading

This is the last editing step and there is no focus on the story itself. The manuscript is considered ready for formatting after this check of keystroke accuracy.

Proofreading includes:

- correcting typing errors such as missed words and misspellings

- standardizing spacing between words and paragraphs

- correcting punctuation

- adherence to rules for capitalization, numbers, italics, and punctuation

Depending on the editor you work with, they may offer to do all three types of editing or specialize in just one. There are also companies that offer to do all three editing types for one lump sum and have different people on staff for each step. Usually the price of garnering all three services at once with one service provider is more economical than going after individual contractors to do each step. Also, longer manuscripts are more negotiable on rates than shorter ones.

Where to Find Editors

If you personally don't know any editors, here are a few ideas as to where you can find these word ninjas.

Word of Mouth

I found the editor I used for my first novel through word of mouth from a fellow indie author. She had been through a few different editors and recommended the one she liked the best. Talk to people in your network to see who they recommend. This is one of the best ways to ensure a good bang for your buck! But, always consider the source. Don't use an editor recommended by an author with poor book reviews.

Professional Organizations

The Editorial Freelancers Association (the-efa.org) is one site with contact information for professional freelance editors and a board for people to post jobs or respond to jobs. Other organizations include the Editors' Association of Canada (www.editors.ca), American Copy Editors Society (copydesk.org), Editorial Freelancers Association (copyediting.com), and National Association of Independent Writers and Editors (naiwe.com).

Depending on the genre, there are author organizations that connect people to professional services as well. For example, the Science Fiction & Fantasy Writers of America (sfwa.org) has many resources for writers to use and some of my contacts told me they found their editors there.

Publishing Houses or Book Distribution Companies

Now that there is a demand for freelance editing services due to the rise of indie publishing, some smaller publishers may not take on your submission, but could loan out their editors for your use instead.

One company I corresponded with was Red Adept Publishing (RedAdeptPublishing.com) who offered editing services for a lump sum. They are an example of a small publisher that offers services to authors instead of a publishing contract. Distribution companies such as Amazon's CreateSpace offer editing services and pricing estimates are available on their website. Some authors on the Amazon forum pointed out that Amazon hires freelance editors for this work and you don't interact with them during the process, so you may want to connect with an editor on your own if you don't want to go through a middle man for every change or question. Also consider that these larger corporations I mentioned tend to focus more on ensuring the margin between what they charge you and what they pay the worker is in the company's favor. This can foster poor quality in the workmanship since cost and profit are the primary consideration.

Freelancer Websites

There are a number of freelance job websites where you can hire all manner of service providers for anything from editing to programming. You can either look up editors or post a job for an editor. Examples of these websites are reedsy.com, fiverr.com, upwork.com, and freelancer.com. Bibliocrunch.com is another site available where one can search for professionals and for a fee, Bibliocrunch staff are available to guide you through the publishing process as well.

Some of these sites have a "bidding" process for the job and it becomes a bidding frenzy as people try to lower their asking price to secure work. Be cautioned that you get what you pay for!

Your Friends and Family

You may also be considering an even cheaper option, which involves the people closest to you. Indie publishing is similar to running a business and be warned that involvement of valuable personal relationships can be detrimental.

However, if you know someone that is a professional editor or has experienced editing and you trust them to do a good job, it could be worth a shot. There are probably strings attached other than price, so just know what you are getting into!

Things to Ask Before Committing to an Editor

During the quoting process, I usually write a polite letter about how I found them and include a few pages of my work for them to look at. The editor will base their pricing on this and will send you a marked up sample to demonstrate their abilities. Be aware that some editors may reject a job if they think they may need to do a lot of corrections. They are editors, not writers, and do not want to rewrite large amounts of text for someone. Also be sure that your document is formatted properly as most editors won't make formatting corrections to documents, but expect them to be a certain standardized format or they may reject working with you. Sometimes coding errors occur when cutting and pasting text between different programs such as between Word and Scrivener. The Authors Helping Authors website has a free Word template available for download that is already set to manuscript submission standard format.

Do take the time to ask them questions before sending any money. Don't be embarrassed or shy! Given that editing can cost a lot of money and you want to be sure you are making a good investment, it is your right and your responsibility to ask questions.

1. *How long have you been an editor and what is your educational and professional background?*

   This question gives you an idea of their experience and what type of work they have done in the past. If they have helped other authors become successful, it bodes well for your future book.

2. *What genres do you specialize in and what genres do you enjoy reading?*

   It may come as a surprise to you, but some editors may refuse to edit some types of material. When I queried for an editor with my vampire fantasy book, I discovered not all editors are willing to read about vampires, and some of them draw the line at material with sex or violence. So make sure the editor is familiar with the genre or the editing will not go well. Unfortunately, as with any field, there are good guys and bad guys. Bad guys will take anything for a buck, no matter the quality being impacted by working on something they don't like or have experience with. I have hired bad editors and needed to tell myself that I can reject the corrections given to me and start over with a better editor. Some of them prey on your insecurities, so stay strong and be confident in your work.

3. *How does this editing process work? How will we communicate?*

People all work in different ways, so it's good to set some expectations in the beginning. Some editors may prefer email communication versus phone conversations. Make sure you are comfortable with the chosen method of communication as you will be working very closely with this person. Inquiring about the pace makes it easier to schedule time for yourself to work on your manuscript. Once I knew that I had to work on at least two chapters every night, I would prepare myself mentally for that after my work day.

Note that editors should be using Track Changes and adding comments instead of overtyping directly in the manuscript and changing everything without your knowledge. It's a collaborative process! They are editing, not rewriting your manuscript. I once had a fairly inexperienced editor dive into my book and rewrite things that made the story nonsensical. An editor's code of ethics must be that they are a guest in your manuscript and all final decisions are yours to make.

4. *How soon can you start editing? Will you be focused on only my project?*

You may be surprised to discover that editing may not happen right away as the editor may be working on other projects. Personally, I like to know that the editor is only working on my manuscript so I don't have to worry about them getting confused between different pieces of work. A good editor will commit to only focusing on your manuscript as standard practice.

5. *Can I divide payments into installments?*

The answer should be yes unless the expense is such a small amount that it's not worth installments. Freelance editors know you are taking a risk on sending money to a stranger and should understand. Do expect editors to require payments be made at the beginning of work periods, versus after, and for no completed work to be sent to you until fulfilled payment schedules have occurred. For example, if the editor agrees to a payment plan of two payments for three weeks of editing work, one would be due at the beginning and the second due halfway through. Just as freelancers should respect our concerns over the risk with sending money out for services, we must respect their efforts to minimize risks of nonpayment or delayed payment.

6. *How will billing and payments be handled?*

PayPal is the preferred method by most providers and offers buyer and seller protection policies. Make sure the approach your editor proposes is up to the professional standard it should be and includes a detailed contract, invoice, and secure payment method.

7. *Random industry questions such as, "Where should I get book reviews after the book is published?"*

These are really questions to see if the editor is up to date with what is happening in the industry. This will help you at a later date when you start selling and marketing because if the editor knows what is going on, they can offer invaluable advice to a self-publishing author.

As mentioned before, a good editor is an incredible find. Over time, you might end up working with more than one editor and this will help you develop your craft. Even if you decide to finish the rest of the publishing steps yourself, at the very least, please spend time with an editor!

Front and Back Matter

After the manuscript is polished up, you will need to add in the front and back matter. A book is basically divided up into three parts: front matter, body of the book (the manuscript), and back matter. Since you are in control of the organization of your book, you can include or not include elements discussed below for the front and back matter. To help you decide, have a look at other books to see what other authors have done.

Front matter elements:

- *Half title page* - This is the first page when you open the book and contains the title of the book. Not all books have this page as sometimes it may be eliminated to keep the book to a shorter page length or specific page number target.

- *Marketing items*– List of other titles and/or blurbs praising the author's works.

- *Frontispiece* - An illustration or decoration which is next to the book's title page.

- *Title page* - Contains information such as the title, subtitle, author name, and publisher.

- *Colophon or Copyright page* - This page includes the copyright notice, publication information, edition information, any cataloguing data, legal notices, ISBN numbers, and sometimes, credits for design, editing, production, and illustration.

- *Dedication* - Books that have a dedication often include this page after the copyright page

- *Epigraph* - This is a quotation, phrase, or poem.

- *Table of contents* - Includes chapter headings, subheadings, and page numbers. Often not applicable as it brings no value to fiction books that don't need reference tools and have generic headings like chapter 1, chapter 2, etc.

- *Foreword* - Usually written by someone other than the author to provide context for the work or provide explanation about an updated edition of the book.

- *Preface* - Written by the author, the preface covers how the book came into being or was developed.

- *Acknowledgement* - Often part of preface to acknowledge those who contributed to the book. Sometimes it is also printed or only printed after the body of the work.

- *Introduction* - The author explains the purpose and goal of the book.

- *Prologue* - This is an opening to a story to establish the setting and give some background details.

The back matter starts after the end of your

manuscript. Elements include:

- *Epilogue* – This part rounds out the design of literary works. Though part of the main story, it occurs after the climax and reveals additional information after the story's ending. It is usually set a few hours later or far in the future, and the writer speaks indirectly through the point of view of a different character.

- *Afterword* – This covers how the book came into being and any last words.

- *Appendix* – Contains supplemental details relevant to the main body of the book.

- *Glossary* – Definitions of industry specific words (like terms used only in astrology or medicine), fictitious words, and other language words used in the book.

- *Bibliography* – Common in nonfiction books, this section cites references used/quoted.

- *Index* – Contains page numbers of where certain terms or subjects can be found within the book. The index takes a lot of time to build and is not a trivial item. Prepare to allocate some time to do this or hire a freelancer to help organize the index if it's a benefit to your book.

After putting together the front matter, edited body of the book, and back matter, the majority of the preparation work is done! As a person who used to paint a lot, I see the completion of the manuscript as equivalent to finishing a painting. The words you use will bring images to life in the reader's mind and it is a piece of art that has come into existence.

Congratulations to you! In a survey conducted by the website thewritepractice.com, it was found that 72% of authors struggle with finishing their book. There's even another staggering statistic floating around that 97% of writers do not finish their books. You have completed a task many others could not finish and you are on your way to becoming an indie author!

3

THE BUSINESS OF SELLING BOOKS

"Believe you can and you're halfway there."

-Theodore Roosevelt

After polishing up your manuscript, you will want to make business structure and product registration decisions before you start formatting your manuscript. These choices position you to finalize the front and back matter, also known as "extra pages," of your manuscript, including the identification number for your copyright page. As well, you may want to think about using a pseudonym to help protect your privacy and if you want to incorporate to separate publishing income from your own personal income.

When you file for copyright registration, apply for an International Standard Book Number (ISBN) or Cataloguing in Publication (CIP data), and be certain to acquire these assignments of permanent, registered identification from the source and avoid discounted or free options. Some sale priced or free registration methods result in you giving some or all of your publishing rights to someone else—nothing is truly free. The ISBN number is what most publishing platforms will require for adding your title to their distribution channels.

What is Copyright?

In the simplest terms, copyright means "the right to copy." In general, this means the owner of the copyright has the sole right to produce or reproduce a work or a substantial part of it in any form. Copyrights apply to everything from artwork, to a lecture, to a book. Of course, any profit derived from the reproduction of this work belongs to the owner of said copyright.

In the chapter about cover creation, book cover art is discussed and you may want to buy the copyright from the artist so you can reproduce the cover freely. If you do not do this, you are obliged to contact the artist for permission to use the image for another purpose than that for which it was originally purchased, such as printing on posters or bookmarks. The artist could charge you a fee every time if they own the copyright. If you have the copyright of the art transferred to you, then you are free to use it for whatever purposes you see fit as you are the copyright owner.

A copyright differs from patents or trademark. Copyrights protect original works of authorship; a patent protects inventions or discoveries; and a trademark protects words, phrases, symbols, or designs identifying the source of the goods or services of one party, distinguishing them from those of others.

Using an example of a video game system, a patent protects the actual invented video game equipment, the video game content is copyrighted, and the system's name brand most likely has a trademarked branding logo. Indie authors own the copyright to their book and may choose to trademark their book series, publishing logo, and any other branding symbols. Most likely you won't be applying for any patents unless you invented something too.

When you create something, you inherently "own" the copyright. However, this world contains people who pirate other people's work for profit. By filing a copyright on your work, you are positioning yourself to use legal recourse to reverse theft and sometimes collect damages in case there is a future lawsuit.

To file for a copyright, you can register online or by mail in most countries and will have to fill in some paperwork and pay a fee. Filing for a copyright is a relatively simple procedure and no matter what country you file in, there are international agreements in place which recognize your filing. As a Canadian, I can file for a copyright in Canada and it will be recognized internationally by countries considered members of the Berne Convention, Universal Copyright Convention, or World Trade Organization (WTO). All the registration sites feature "how to" guides with directions on how to fill out their forms and submit your manuscript and payment.

The Canadian Intellectual Property Office (ic.gc.ca) deals with copyright filing in Canada. Prior to filing for a copyright, you must open an Industry Canada account, which is free. There is an option to file online ($50 CDN) or by snail mail ($65CDN).

The US Copyright office (copyright.gov) charges $35 USD for a basic copyright application. Prices go up for paper applications and there are other options, such as paying $115 USD to protect an unpublished piece of work.

The UK Intellectual Property Office (gov.uk/government/organisations/intellectual-property-office) does not have an official registration system; it's assumed that the creator owns the copyright. However, there are various private companies that maintain a copyright database for a fee if one wants to register with them to create an unquestionable record if you fear needing it in court one day.

If your book features artwork for which you own the copyright, you can use the formatted book (completed manuscript with art in place) for your application to have them included in your official record. Because this commissioned art work comes with a contract that states transfer of title, you already have a record that is submissible in court to prove ownership. You can also register the art with the copyright office on an individual basis, paying a fee for each piece of art when a book has more than just cover art, or in a publication of its own called a "compilation." This way you have an officially registered certificate of copyright for each piece of art if there ever is a dispute.

Once you create something, the copyright is yours until you sell it, trade it, give it away, or die. You can will a copyrighted work to a beneficiary so they may profit from future royalties. Just remember to do this before you leave this planet.

What is an ISBN?

The acronym ISBN stands for International Standard Book Number. This is a unique number code created for booksellers and has evolved over time from 9 digits to the present day 13 digits. Both 10 and 13 digit numbers are provided for each title as some systems still have 10 digit fields in their forms. This number is used in ordering systems by book stores, internet retailers, and libraries.

The ISBN is country specific and usually authors have to buy the ISBN number for their books. The International ISBN Agency website (isbn-international.org) has information and listings about where you can obtain an ISBN appropriate to your country.

If you decide to publish different formats (also known as versions) of your book such as an eBook, paperback, hard back, and audio book, you will need four ISBNs; one for each format.

Due to economic reasons, many indie authors choose to accept a distributor's free ISBN. However, the distributor becomes listed as the publisher since they paid for the ISBN. Any reseller looking up the book will direct purchasing inquiries to the distributor and not to you since that is the information listed with the ISBN. If you publish on multiple platforms, it will appear as if your book is published by different distributors instead of one publisher: you. When you purchase an ISBN from the source and use it with all distributor sites, you will always appear as the publisher and any inquiries will be directed to the contact information you put on the record for that number.

In Canada, the government agency Library and Archives Canada (bac-lac.gc.ca) is the responsible entity for ISBN distribution at no cost to Canadian citizens. All you have to do is visit their website and register for an account. After account activation, you can request an ISBN for whatever format of book you want to produce.

For US residents, the privately held company RR Bowker (bowker.com) distributes ISBNs. One number will cost $125 USD and there are super discounts if you buy in bulk, such as a block of 10 ISBNs for $295 USD or 100 for $575 USD. Sign up for your free account before you need an ISBN number at myidentifiers.com and sometimes they send out marketing emails offering sale prices on blocks of numbers—the sooner you establish that free account, the better the chance for getting a better deal on numbers you will need in the future anyway.

It is similar in the United Kingdom and Ireland. A

privately held company, Nielsen Book Services (isbn.nielsenbook.co.uk) will sell you ISBNs in lots of 10 for £126.00 or 100 ISBNs for £294.00.

While the costs seem daunting to purchase ISBNs, in the long run you will have more control over your titles and may be contacted for reselling opportunities. Industry professionals will also take you more seriously as you are investing in your budding writing career.

How to Create a Free ISBN Barcode

After obtaining an ISBN, you will need to generate a graphic for your book's back cover (print book) or end page (eBook). The ISBN information will also be included as part of your front matter's copyright page.

Doing a general search online will yield many options for ISBN barcode generation. Basically, you type your ISBN into a website and press a button to create an ISBN barcode image, which you can then save. Sometimes you are given the option of adding a price to the image as well. A free barcode generator that includes options of different DPI resolution, hyphens, price, and file formats is available at bookow.com.

What is CIP?

CIP stands for Cataloguing in Publication, which is a voluntary program of cooperation between publishers and libraries. Books are assigned basic cataloging data (CIP record) for inclusion in the country's National Library catalogue. Usually the CIP record is included near the bottom of the copyright page. Each National Library maintains a database of entries that it creates. CIP records are not provided to individual authors—creating a corporation to publish your books would qualify you to apply for a CIP record as a publisher. Also, your book must have an ISBN that you own directly and not through another publisher.

In Canada, the CIP record is created by Library and Archives Canada (bac-lac.gc.ca). The record is provided free of charge for any publication with a print run of at least 100 copies. After filling in the application form, the CIP record will take a minimum of 15 working days for completion of cataloging, then is emailed to you. After the indicated publication date, the publisher will receive a letter requesting a hard copy of the book to be sent to the Canadian National library for archiving. The eBook can also be archived online.

The Library of Congress (loc.gov) in the US is the institute that provides the CIP record. The Library will only provide CIP records for a publisher that has already published a minimum of three titles by three different authors. There is no charge for the CIP record and they strive to provide the data after three weeks. After publishing, a copy of the book should be sent to the library for archiving.

The British National Bibliography (bnb.bl.uk) provides CIP free of charge as well, and needs at least four months for CIP record creation. A copy of the book should be mailed to the British Library post publication.

Many indie authors do not bother to apply for CIP records since it is not a necessary step for publishing. Having a CIP record enables libraries to look up your book, and archiving a physical copy of your book in the library leaves a legacy.

Pseudonym Considerations

Historically, many writers have used pseudonyms, or pen names, for various reasons. Your writing could interfere with your career. You may have heard of people getting fired from their jobs or ridiculed by colleagues for writing erotica under their real name. Even if your friends and families know you are a writer, having some privacy outside of your immediate circle is a good thing.

For some authors, such as JK Rowling, using a pseudonym allowed her to cross genres. She became so well known for writing young adult fiction, that after finishing an adult novel, she released it under the name of Robert Galbraith to avoid disappointing reader expectations.

In the future, you may also gain super fans. Having any fans is pretty flattering; however, sometimes fans can turn into super obsessed stalkers. Using a pseudonym can make it very difficult for strangers to learn who you are and where you live, and allow you to keep your writing persona separate from the rest of your life.

Pros and Cons of Incorporating

Some authors choose to incorporate in order to keep income from their book sales separate from their main income. This is an option that will require much paperwork and annual income tax filings. It is a lot of work to open up a business even if it doesn't generate much revenue!

Incorporating is a personal decision. Many self-published authors are not incorporated and simply claim the book profits as part of their main income. Establishing and managing a corporation will incur expenses and you have to compare this to your projected sales to determine if this step is worth doing.

Pros:

- *Limited liability* – An LLC structure for your publishing company separates it as a legal entity, so any creditors or legal actions against your corporation's assets cannot consider your personal income or assets. As well, any debt incurred and revenue generated belongs to the corporation, not the owners.

- *Sole Proprietor* – This structure is simplest and allows the proprietor to handle tax reporting as self-employed, adding several reports to their annual filing process. The owner is also personally responsible for the business's income and expenses, and creditors and legal actions.

- *Taxes* – You gain the ability to claim tax deductions on items such as salaries, incentive compensations, and fringe benefits in an LLC. Expenses related to penning your book, such as research or office supplies; all of the publishing services and your home office space, in addition to other deductions, can be written off in either case.

- *Access to capital* – Financial institutions are more comfortable providing loans to a corporation with a current business plan. As well, shares can be set up to attract outside investment.

Cons:

- *Fees* – Incorporating will cost money. Although you can do it yourself, it would be best to have the help of a lawyer and an accountant unless you can bring that expertise to the table. Filing and professional fees for starting an incorporation can range from $1,000-$3,000.

- *Lots of paperwork* – You will need to keep records of all transactions, maintain separate tax returns, and create articles of incorporation.

- *Taxes* – Filing annual income tax returns can be costly due to accounting fees. If a one person business incorporates, any revenue the owner generates is taxed twice, first at the corporate level, then again on their personal income tax return.

Incorporating requires a lot of careful planning and expert advice. You do not need to incorporate to indie publish, and can do so at a later date. In the US, over 70% of businesses are owned by sole proprietors and operate without incorporating to the level of a more structured Limited Liability Company. Most ecommerce merchants like people selling on eBay, for example, would probably not go through the hassles of incorporation.

If you do decide to incorporate, look up information specific to your country. Local business bureaus or associations provide a lot of free resources that can help guide the way. Different countries have different corporate structure options such as Sole Proprietorship, Partnership, Cooperative, Limited Liability Company, Corporation, S Corporation, and so on. Each structure has its own advantages and disadvantages depending on what your needs are. You should consider hiring a lawyer to sort through legal requirements and documentation if you feel uncertain about how to incorporate.

Creating a business and managing it on an ongoing basis is an addition to your already full plate. Incorporating is optional and not doing it won't stop you from publishing. The choice is up to you!

DISTRIBUTION AND ROYALTIES

"The story of the human race is the story of men and women selling themselves short."

-Abraham Maslow

What is Distribution?

Distribution is making your book available for purchase. In the beginning, you may get some support from your family and friends to shell over some dollars for your books. However, for continuous sales, you will need to do some distribution and marketing work to earn revenue from strangers. The distribution company will take a cut in exchange for printing and fulfilling orders for your book through retailers. Retailers are online websites and brick and mortar stores who will also take a cut for selling your books to customers. Whatever is left after distribution and retailer cuts is your hard earned royalty income. Don't sell yourself short and think no one will buy your book. Have confidence that readers will discover you and support your work by purchasing it!

To sell your book through different retailers, you choose a distributor and sign a contract with them. The barrier for entry is low cost, or free in some cases. Most of the major distributors are US based companies who cater globally. If you are not a resident of the US, there are some tax implications as the IRS will automatically deduct 30% off collected royalties. We will cover how to avoid that penalty at the end of this chapter.

After choosing a distributor, you must format the book according to their requirements. Distributors differ according to how many retailers are part of their network, fee for services, and royalty percentages. Some distributors will only help you sell eBooks while others deal with both print and eBooks, so you could end up working with more than one. Keep in mind that if you have more than one distributor, they may be supplying the same retailers. Before signing the contract, look into whether you can opt out of individual retail channels to prevent overlap.

Differences Between Print and eBook Distribution

One of the biggest differences between print and eBook distribution is the cost of producing the book. Print books have smaller profit margins due to cost of paper, printing, mailing, and labor. EBooks have server storage costs, but overall you will receive a higher profit margin compared to a print book. For example, you can earn $3 in royalties on the sale of an eBook versus $0.30 on a print book.

Generally, eBooks are much cheaper and easier to distribute on a global basis since it involves online retailers rather than brick and mortar stores. There are no real boundaries in regards to where you can sell your eBook, and as an indie author, you have much more freedom than a traditional publisher who may have complicated international rights agreements.

For print books, getting directly into large chain bookstores is difficult for any indie author because all the shelf space has been committed to large publishing companies. According to outthinkgroup.com, a book (regardless of how it was published) has less than a 1% chance of being stocked in an average bookstore.

While talking to a magazine publisher about how difficult it was to get an indie book into a bookstore, he told me this: "There is a fine line between traditional publishing and self-publishing. And that line is made up of money." Citing an example of magazines displayed in convenience store windows, he pointed out that all those spots had been paid for. If I had a couple of thousand dollars to throw around, he was certain it would be possible to obtain some shelf space in a large chain bookstore. However, it is unlikely an indie author would have the budget to do this. Instead, we will look at other methods such as consignment deals with smaller stores and choosing a distributor that can put our work into catalogues so people can visit a large bookstore to order your book.

To land your book into smaller, independently owned book stores, you typically approach the owner and ask if they are interested in carrying your book. You may have to do a sales pitch and explain why your book is a good fit for their store. Many indie book stores have websites and provide requirements and forms for you to request a place on their shelves via email. One deal I had with a book store was to supply them with ten books and split the retail price 50-50. Since you are setting the price, you will have to consider how much it costs to print the books and make sure you create a profit margin that allows for discount percentages.

For example, the standard discount for bookstores is typically 40% of your book's retail price. If your book sells for $10, you can subtract 40% off the price ($4.00) for the bookstore's share, and you will get 60% for each book sold ($6.00).

Consignment selling takes a lot of time as you have to approach each store individually, but you will get your book into some stores as a result. Sadly, this method is not without risk; one of the bookstores I worked with went bankrupt and the owner disappeared. The books were written off as a loss…the cost of doing business.

All book stores and libraries order books via catalogues from companies such as Ingram Sparks, Nielsen, and Baker & Taylor. If a distributor has the option of distributing print books, they usually have a print on demand (POD) service and will list the title in different catalogues for eBooks and print books. This means people visiting bookstores can order your book even though it is not stocked on their shelves. After the order is placed through the catalogue, the distributor will print a copy of the book and send it to the bookstore for the customer. This POD service also allows authors to sell their book through all of the distributor's retail channels without storing inventory in their basement. Not all distributors have catalogue access, so read up on their retailer's terms and conditions to find out.

Be aware some bookstores tend to have return policies for their customers. When a customer returns a book, the publisher will have to pay for the book to be destroyed or returned to them since it has been "used." These are established rules and risks traditional publishers have agreed to for many years before you entered the market, and a common reason why indie books aren't stocked. Indie authors tend to choose the "no return" option in the data for their books, which transfers the risk to bookstores if a customer wants to return a book. If you do allow returns, you will be responsible for paying for their destruction or for shipping costs to have the book mailed to you.

The latest Pew Internet Research study shows that e-reading in the US is on the rise and the percentage of American adults who read eBooks in the past year was 28% in 2014, up from 11% in 2011. The same study shows the percentage of people who have read print books in the past year was 69% in 2014, which is down slightly from 71% in 2011. Although eBooks are more popular with younger readers, it is obvious that print is still very much alive and worth the trouble to have this product version available to market.

What are Royalties?

Royalties are the profits you gain from the sale of the book after distributors and retailers take their cut. If you print a book, it is the profit after the cost of printing and distribution. For an eBook, it is the profit after the cost charged for storing the book on a server and making the book available for download. Royalty agreements are different for each distributor and there is usually a clause that rules can be changed even after you sign an agreement for a certain royalty rate.

Indie publishing gives you the most control over royalty information as the author has direct access to the sales data at any given time. Traditional publishers and vanity presses can give reports on the sales after their analysis, but the author will never have access to any data.

In a perfect world, a royalty on your book can be calculated this way:

Retail List Price - Book Distributor & Retailer Fees = Your Royalty Amount

If you sold your book at a retail price of $1.00 with 70% royalty rate and no fees, the book distributor will take $0.30 for their services and you will end up with $0.70. In reality, there are lots of little charges for distribution services, therefore you will most likely not receive $0.70. Book distributor fees cover the costs of printing and distribution. Retailer fees is the cut retailers take when someone orders your book from a catalogue through them.

The way royalties are calculated for eBooks and print books are a bit different. For both types of books, the country of the purchaser can come into play and if there is any price matching, your royalty will be lower. The equation on royalties is really:

Sale Price - Book Distributor & Retailer Fees - Delivery Costs - Matching Costs = Your Royalty Amount

The "sale price" is the listed purchase price. Although you do pick the retail price of your book, the distributor can modify the price based on different factors. For example, you decide to run a $0.99 promotion at one online retailer site while it costs $1.99 on another site. Through the magic of the internet, the second online retailer with the $1.99 priced book will automatically change the retail list price of your book to $0.99 or lower to match their competitor. The difference between $1.99 and the final sale price is the matching cost. Delivery costs can be eBook storage server costs or price of shipping print book to customer.

In the contract you have with each distributor, you may see that they have the right to change the price of your book at any time. Sometimes it is worth the trouble to check on your book page once in a while to ensure the price is set correctly.

Each distributor may calculate royalties differently, and they usually have a FAQ page or online calculator to help you understand their method. As well, royalties are often held back until a certain threshold is reached as it is not worth it for the distributor to process payments for multiple small amounts of money. This means that if you don't sell a certain number of books, you may never see your share of royalties!

How to Price Your Book

Before you start selling anything, you will have to determine a price. Books are no different. You may have noticed that doing anything for a print book requires a bit more thinking and is more complicated than eBooks. This applies to price setting as well.

Pricing Print Books

Since print books cost more to produce, the price will have to be higher than an eBook. If multiple parties are involved in distribution, the royalty can be net negative if the price is set too low. Usually the distribution site will not allow you to set a print book price that will create a loss for each sale.

To keep costs down, you can do a few things:

- Consider the paper type as this may increase the print cost of the book.

- Choosing a larger size book will mean less pages to print.

- Adjust your trim size or font details for less total pages (but not too much or the book will be hard to read, or too different to be appealing).

- Don't have any interior color pages unless you need them because a few pages of color costs the same as printing the entire book in color.

- If you intend to sell books in person, there may be

discounts on multiple copies and you can save on shipping costs.

Pricing eBooks

You can pretty much choose any price and even give eBooks away for free. Be aware that free or lower priced books are not valued by readers as much as paid books, although this low barrier to entry may attract more people to try your work.

Over time, eBook prices of bestsellers have been on the decline according to a Pew Research Center study, from $12.00 USD in 2012 to $8.00 USD in 2014. Even if you don't think your book will make it onto the best seller list, remember readers have a choice between buying your book or a bestseller. Setting a high price could yield a higher royalty percentage, however, setting a lower price could help you sell more units and overall, make more profit. Nothing from a higher price point is still nothing, while something from a lower price point is profit.

After selecting a distributor, see if they have an online calculator to help you calculate costs. Otherwise, you will have to calculate the royalty manually or wait until a sale happens to see how the breakdown occurred. As mentioned before, the distributor has the right to change the price at any time, so check your book page as the sale price will directly affect your royalties.

To help you figure out how to price your eBook, I recommend looking online for the latest information. One good site is authorearnings.com, which analyzes Amazon data monthly. Smashwords offered a great analysis on eBooks sold on their website in 2013, which found that $2.99 USD was the most commonly set price point. If you price the eBook too low, you won't gain much profit and if you price it too high, you may not sell enough. The happy medium appears to be a price between $2.80 - $4.00 USD according to this survey.

A really good analysis on eBook pricing by David Gaughran is available on his author blog and website (davidgaughran.wordpress.com/basics/pricing/) in which he outlines how he decided on this pricing structure for his works. His prices are $0.99 USD for short story singles, $2.99 USD for a five story collection, and $4.99 USD for a ten story collection or full length novel.

If you have a long book you may want to choose a higher price point. For my first novel, the word count was close to 120,000, so I decided on a price point of $4.99 USD. The distributor would adjust the price equivalent to whatever currency the reader is based in. I found out that I could not set a $4.99 CDN and $4.99 USD price point at the same time to give Canadian readers a break. In the end, I settled on $4.99 USD.

Price is only one factor in the success of a book, which is why it is important to continue marketing and seeking out new ways to find new readers. It is also something you can change at a later date, and pricing your book will depend on how the market is doing along with any changes in your writing career. For instance, you may set your book first at $4.99 USD and then choose to give it away later when the second book comes up, to promote sales.

Distribution Options

To start the distribution process, sign up for an online account and then digitally sign a contract, which includes many details, such as the fact that you own the copyright to the book. The world of distribution is small and you will discover many distributors will send your book to the same retail channels. For common channels, you will usually have the option to opt out of them to avoid overlaps. You will have to make the decision on which distributor you want to use for these common channels.

For example, you can open an account with Apple Inc to distribute your eBook and they will pay you royalties directly. However, when you open an account with the distributor Smashwords, they also distribute to Apple. Most likely you would choose not to distribute your eBook through Smashwords to Apple readers as Smashwords would take a cut of your royalties along with Apple. However, there are authors that prefer the convenience of Smashwords handling all retail channels instead of opening multiple accounts directly with retailers. It may also be easier to collect royalties as you might not reach the threshold for royalty payments through Apple alone. Since Smashwords is an aggregator of retail channels, you could sell enough in several places for Smashwords to issue your royalties.

When choosing a distributor, be aware that some only distribute eBooks and no print books, while others do both print and eBooks, and the quality of your product varies from one to the next. Some do not charge any fees for distribution while others do. One example of a free service is Amazon Kindle Direct Publishing and they make their money by taking a cut of royalties. A distributor who charges set up fees is Ingram Spark. They are the biggest POD company in the world with over 39,000 outlets, and are known for exceptional print and binding quality. They take a larger cut of royalties than Amazon as well. What justifies the cost of using Ingram Spark is their large distribution reach, which includes brick and mortar bookstores via catalogues as well as most of the eBook retailers.

A few distributors will claim you can keep 100% of your royalties, but you have to buy a package from them to get that benefit as part of their services. They make their money upfront, which essentially pays for their royalty share immediately. Before committing to any packages, check out their list of retail channels. There is a good chance they are the same as a distributor who doesn't charge any money for the same channels.

There is no right or wrong way to do this and you can choose multiple distributors or try your luck with just one. It was a bit disheartening when I discovered that some of the distributors are not giving out a listing of all their retail channels. This makes it difficult to compare distributors, and over the years, it appears many of them are partnering up with each other so each of them will get a cut of your royalties.

Here are a few select distributors which are very popular with indie authors. Visit their website for the latest information. Be aware that you can switch between distributors, however, you risk losing book reviews as these don't move with changes in sales listings.

Smashwords (smashwords.com)

Smashwords is an online eBook self-publishing company founded by Mark Coker in 2008. He is quite an active speaker and gives a lot of talks on indie publishing. Smashwords has a retail channel on their website and can also upload your book to other channels.

- *Price for using:* Free

- *Titles available:* 372,311+

- *Book format:* only eBooks

- *File types accepted:* Microsoft Word, Open Office Word doc, or ePub

- *Distribution reach:* Your book will be uploaded to Apple iBooks, Barnes & Noble, Kobo, OverDrive, Flipkart, Oyster, Scribd, Baker & Taylor's Blio, Axis 360, and more.

- *Support:* Contact form only

- *Royalty rate:* Promises 80% for books sold on

Smashwords site and about 60% from other sites (Smashwords takes roughly 10% commission and retailer commission varies). You will be paid once your earnings are over $10 USD for electronic payment and $75 USD for paper checks. As well, you need to ensure that your book format is good enough for wider distribution in their premium catalogue to access all their retail channels. Their website has a list with all the reasons why a file is rejected for their premium catalogue and tips on how to get in.

- *Author tools:* coupons, pre-ordering of book before release, free books on publishing & marketing, author page, self-interview page, blog with tips.

- *Pro:* It's one of the world's largest indie eBook distributors (other is Amazon) and offers daily sales reporting. Once you upload your file into their "meat grinder" program, it will convert your one file into multiple files for all the different retailers. Smashwords offers many free guides to authors on publishing and marketing as they want you to be successful in order for them to earn their commission. You can also opt in or out of specific distribution channels. It may be easier to collect a royalty check due to aggregated sales.

- *Cons:* Giving up 10% of your royalties to use their service. If you have a new version of the book, it will take awhile to update all the retail channels. Sales data may not be up to date since they have to wait for retailers to give them the information.

Draft2Digital (draft2digital.com)

Founded in 2012, Draft2Digital is a much smaller company than Smashwords and prides itself on offering a simple, user friendly distribution experience.

- *Price for using:* Free

- *Titles available:* 50,000+

- *Book formats:* eBooks and paperbacks

- *File types accepted:* Word doc, rich text format (RTF), and ePub

- *Distribution reach:* Your book will be uploaded to Apple iBooks, Barnes & Noble, Kobo, Scribd, Page Foundry, Tolino, Oyster, and CreateSpace.

- *Support:* Email, contact form, and phone

- *Royalty rate:* Typically you would get 60%, but it depends on retail channel costs. Monthly payments will be made after minimum threshold is reached, $25 USD for checks and $10 USD for digital payments.

- *Author tools:* blog with tips on publishing and marketing.

- *Pro:* Similar to Smashwords, you upload one file for formatting and distribution. You can also opt in or opt out of specific distribution channels if you already have accounts with certain retailers. It's been reported by some authors that the customer support is very good from this distributor.

- *Cons:* The distribution list is small compared to Smashwords and there will be a wait for real time data. Also, there aren't many free tools.

Lulu (lulu.com)

Established in 2002, one of the company's co-founders is Bob Young, a serial entrepreneur who had a bad experience trying to publish his own book. Offshoots of Lulu include Lulu Jr, which allows children to become published authors, and Replay Photos, which offers professional photography of sports.

- *Price for using:* Free and several paid packages are available for print and eBooks

- *Titles available:* 2,000,000+

- *Book formats:* eBooks, paperbacks, and hardcovers

- *File types accepted:* lots of different file types ranging from .doc to .gif

- *Distribution reach:* Your book will be uploaded to Apple iBooks, Barnes & Noble, Kobo, Amazon, and the Ingram Spark network.

- *Support:* Contact form

- *Royalty rate:* For print books, the royalty rate is roughly 30% when sold through Lulu's website, or 5% through other retailers. EBook royalties range from 38% when sold through other retailers, to 77% through Lulu. A royalty calculator is available at http://www.lulu.com/distribution/sell.php for more precise information. Monthly payment will be made after minimum threshold is reached, $20 USD for checks and $5 USD for digital payments.

- *Author tools:* forum for asking questions, guidebooks for publishing and marketing, and how to videos.

- *Pro:* Printing hardcover books is available as an option. Can list your book in the Ingram Spark catalogue for free without paying annual fees, although it is uncertain if this would be the same as paying for the service directly through Ingram Spark. I contacted Lulu about this to see if it was true. It was confirmed that if I request for the book to be included in the Ingram catalogue, I would be the publisher listed and not Lulu. But I have not tried this method, so I really don't know what the catch is. They also have an easy to use online royalty tool.

- *Cons:* Same as others that aggregate to multiple retailers; if a book has to be re-uploaded, there will be a lag. This applies to sales data as well.

Amazon

Amazon has three subsidiary arms for publishing: Amazon Kindle for eBooks, Amazon CreateSpace for print books, and Amazon ACX for audiobooks. ACX is only available for residents of the United States or United Kingdom who hold a valid US or UK Taxpayer Identification Number. CreateSpace is also in the business of selling print on demand CDs and DVDs if you want to expand your artistic vision.

Over the years, there have been many negative things said about Amazon, however, having the easiest and most user friendly platform for indie publishing available online has made them the largest. Since so many people sell and buy on Amazon, there are a variety of opinions, so it's no wonder negativity exists and is heard about this industry giant. Note that Amazon holds the spot for selling the most eBooks over all other retailers with some stats estimating they have 60% of the eBook market.

If you decide to publish Kindle, print, and audio books via Amazon, you will need to open three separate accounts as they are separate entities. When you log onto each website, you can be confident that you are applying the changes to one version versus another. For example, you may be updating the Kindle version with extra artwork, but not on the CreateSpace paperback version due to color printing costs.

Amazon also lets authors create their own author page and link their biography, blog, website, and sales listings to encourage fan behaviors. To create this page, open an account at https://authorcentral.amazon.com. The author page also shows all the books you've published, which can help a consumer find more of your books once they discover the first one.

Amazon Kindle Direct Publishing (kdp.amazon.com)

- *Price for using:* Free

- *Titles available:* 3,600,000+

- *Book format:* distributes eBooks in Kindle .mobi format only

- *File types accepted:* Word doc, rich text format (RTF), pdf, mobi, html, and ePub

- *Distribution reach:* Your book will only be sold on Amazon and you can control which countries.

- *Support:* Contact form

- *Royalty rate:* The royalty rate is 35-70% depending on options you pick (related to delivery costs, taxes, etc.) and where the consumer lives. Bi-monthly digital payments with no thresholds or $100 USD by check.

- *Author tools:* Amazon author page; email newsletters with author interviews, writing, and marketing advice; community forum with tips; and Kindle countdown/free day promo tool available only if you choose to exclusively sell on Amazon for 90 days (this can be renewed more than once).

- *Pro:* User friendly software for uploading and cover creation. Very clear help section with specific instructions. The royalty rate is fairly high and no thresholds on digital payment means you will be paid much quicker. Sales data is almost real time, which is pretty amazing. Note that Amazon offers free software: KindleGen (file conversion) and Kindle Previewer (mobi file previewer) to help you create and test your book files. Building Your Book for Kindle is also available for free to guide you step by step on how to create and upload your files for distribution.

- *Cons:* Distribution is limited to Amazon sites only. The Kindle countdown or free day tool can only be used once during every 90 day period. If your book is discovered for sale on another website during the countdown, Amazon will not sell the book.

Amazon CreateSpace (createspace.com)

- *Price for using:* Free

- *Titles available:* 2,000,000+

- *Book format:* paperbacks

- *File types accepted:* PDF

- *Distribution reach:* If you choose extended distribution, your book is available to bookstores, online retailers, libraries, and academic institutions. I emailed to ask for a list of retailers and was told it was not available.

- *Support:* Contact form and phone

- *Royalty rate:* Amazon cites examples that it would roughly be 20%, but there are many factors such as sales channel percentage, fixed charge, and per-page charge. The best way to calculate your royalty is by using their online calculator at createspace.com/Products/Book/Royalties.jsp. Payment by check will be made after minimum threshold of $100 USD is reached. Direct deposit with no threshold is available only for the US, UK, Germany, France, Spain, Portugal, Belgium, Austria, and the Netherlands.

- *Author tools:* links with Amazon author page; email

newsletters with author interviews, writing, and marketing advice; how to videos and community forum with tips.

- *Pro:* Offers some of the best prices for printing a paperback book which helps increase profit margin. Great calculator for estimating royalty rate. User friendly software for uploading and cover creation. Very clear help section with good instructions.

- *Cons:* Not sure what retailers will be selling your book, although you have the option of only selling on Amazon. Unless you earn a minimum royalty of $100, you may never see your money! Also you cannot create hardcover books. Bookstores may decline to carry a product with an exclusive Amazon relationship due to competition issues. Information in wholesale catalogues do indicate who the printer is for a book.

Amazon ACX (acx.com)

- *Price for using:* Free to open an account, fees for narrator and audio producer if any are hired

- *Titles available:* 40,543+

- *Book format:* audio books

- *File types accepted:* mp3

- *Distribution reach:* Your audio book will be uploaded to Audible, Amazon, and iTunes

- *Support:* Contact form, email, and phone

- *Royalty rate:* Ranges from 25-40% depending on retailer and audio book length. They sometimes run incentive programs such as the $50 USD Bounty Payment, which gives $50 to the author for any new Audible listener who downloads their book. Paid monthly after threshold of $10 USD is reached for direct deposit or $50 USD by check.

- *Author tools:* free software for authors who want to narrate their own books, help section with lots of links on marketing and audio book creation.

- *Pro:* Another earning opportunity for your book!

- *Cons:* Only open to United States residents, United Kingdom residents, and people who hold a valid US or UK Taxpayer Identification Number. You may also want to invest in sound equipment, which is another expense to add to your list.

Ingram Spark (ingramspark.com)

Ingram is the world's largest book distributor with over 50 years in the business. They are a huge company with offices all over the world. Typically, traditional publishers use their services.

• Price for using: $49 USD for uploading either print book only or one print version and eBook at the same time ($49 USD refunded if 50 print copies ordered within 60 days) and $12 USD per title per year for catalogue maintenance

- *Titles available:* 7,500,000+

- *Book formats:* eBooks, paperbacks, and hardcovers

- *File types accepted:* PDF and ePub

- *Distribution reach:* Over 39,000 retailers and libraries

- *Support:* Contact form and phone

- *Royalty rate:* For eBooks - 40-45%, print books - 40-70% after printing costs; calculator available at ingramspark.com/Portal/Calculators/PubCompCa lculator. There doesn't appear to be a threshold for monthly payments.

- *Author tools:* video learning series, FAQ, file creation guides and templates, calculators, publisher guide.

- *Pro:* Ingram is the biggest book distributor in the world, so you would be putting your book into all outlets possible, including Amazon. They are also known for exceptional quality products and preferred by most brick and mortar vendors. It's easy and inexpensive to get into their wholesale catalogue, which goes to the major bookstores and libraries.

- *Cons:* Cost of upload and annuals fees for life of the book if you choose to include it in the wholesale catalogue. If you discover mistakes and need to re-upload the book, you will need to pay a file change fee to do so each time. This company caters to professionals in the industry and expects indie author clients to have the same skill sets as the professionals, so customer service is not helpful like someone learning might expect.

Popular Online Retailers for eBooks

Listed here are popular online sites for eBooks where you can open an account directly for uploading and selling your book. These sites are called "single channel distribution" because they only sell your book on their site. The distributors previously mentioned were aggregate retail channels for "multiple channel distribution"—they sell your book on their site and upload it to other sites. It's up to you if you want to open an account with these single channel distributors or choose to go through a multiple site distributor to maintain one account instead of multiple accounts.

Single channel distributors include:

- *Kobo* (kobo.com/writinglife)

- *Apple iBooks* (apple.com/itunes/working-itunes/sell-content/books)

- *Nook* (www.nookpress.com/ebooks), when I checked in August 2015, Canadians were not allowed to self-publish directly with them

- *Google Books* (play.google.com/books/publish)

- *Tolino* (tolino-media.de) for German books

Your head may be hurting after reading about so many distribution options. Mine certainly was as I tried to make the best decision for my books! If you want to test the waters, start by uploading your eBook and print book to Amazon. They have great software and if you make a mistake, there is no cost to upload a revised document (no extra fees and minimal lag time). If you make a mistake on print pricing, they will point out that each sale is a loss and will not permit you to sell unless you increase the price. The sales data for KDP is almost real time, with a lag between 2-4 hours—pretty impressive. The resources available to help with formatting and uploading are decent. With so many authors using Amazon, there is no shortage of information available on any question you may have.

In the future, your readers may start influencing your distribution decisions when they start asking about where to buy your book as they may use other types of e-readers or expect to be able to order your book in bookstores. Changing distributors is always an option, but remember that there is a risk of losing book reviews and/or sales momentum because this is major disruption to selling.

What is Metadata?

When you start reading more about indie publishing, you will encounter a term called metadata over and over again. Basically, it's the technical information you type in when you upload to a distributor. It's important the information is accurate and no mistakes are made, otherwise it will be difficult for readers to track your book down.

Metadata includes items such as:

- *Book Title* - The title is the most frequently searched item. When you fill in the title field of your book, it must be the same title appearing on your book's cover and spine. Missing title information will confuse search engines, so when someone looks up your book it would not show up near the top of results.

- *Subtitle* - The title and subtitle combined must be fewer than 200 characters.

- *Series Title* - This only applies if the book is part of a series. If not, then the field is left blank. This item allows customers to search for all the books related to each other in a series if the information is filled in for each book title.

- *ISBN* - If you have an ISBN you can enter it, otherwise the distributor can assign their own ISBN number to your book if you choose to use their free one.

- *Description* - This can be the same as the blurb or synopsis you have written for your print book back cover. Generally, it's about 150 words and gives a hint of the plot to excite potential readers.

- *Author Biography* - Some distributors will ask for biographical information to be shared with consumers.

- *Category* - This is a really important field as your book will be ranked within categories of similar books. Some authors choose niche categories with fewer titles, making it easier to move up the ranks when their book sales increase. However, if the category is too narrow, then it makes it hard to sell books if no one can find them.

- *Contributors* - There are additional fields that identify the book's author, editor, illustrator, translator, and others who deserve credit. To publish a book at least one contributor name is required, so at minimum, the author must be listed. If you have created an Amazon author page, the author credit will link to this page if you are selling on Amazon and only if the spelling is exactly the same, including middle initial, if any.

- *Keywords* - For each book, you can compile a list of keywords or a phrase (preferably 2-3 words long) to help readers search for your book. These also contribute to the sales ranking categories, so researching similar books on Amazon or other online retailers can help you determine the best keywords for yours.

If you are thinking about publishing more than one book, it would help to have a file of the metadata you entered to ensure consistency as you will be asked some of the same questions on every publishing site and some will be the same from one book to the next. For example, in a series, keywords and categories should match. Filling in so many fields may seem tedious, but it will help your book sales in the long run, so do spend some time doing it.

Tax Consideration for Non-US Citizens

Since most distribution companies are US based companies, they will automatically deduct 30% of royalties for the Internal Revenue Service (IRS). If you do not do the paperwork to avoid this, there will be double taxation because your country will tax your royalties as income and the IRS would have already taken 30%.

To solve this issue, you need to apply for an ITIN (Individual Taxpayer Identification Number), which is a tax processing number issued by the IRS to people who have a reason to not pay US taxes.

To get an ITIN:

1. Go to IRS website (irs.gov) for latest information and fill in form W-7.

2. Decide which of the 13 acceptable documents you will send to IRS to prove your foreign status. Be aware you may need to line up at the passport office to obtain certified copies of your passport to start this process.

3. Visit a US embassy or overseas public accounting firm for form processing, or mail the form to the IRS.

It takes eight weeks for the IRS to process paperwork. If they are late, they will send you a letter to let you know that your application has been received and they are working on it.

After getting the ITIN number, fill in a form with each distributor and ask them to submit it to the IRS on your behalf to release 30% of your royalties in order for you to declare the full amount of royalties earned as income to pay taxes in your own country.

For publishing corporations that are non-US based, an Employer Identification Number (EIN) is required for exemption from the same 30% IRS deduction on royalties.

To get an EIN:

1. Go to IRS website (irs.gov) for latest information and fill in form Form SS-4 or call

them directly to apply by phone. It is not a toll free number.

2.   A letter will be sent in the mail from the IRS to provide you with the EIN.

After receiving the EIN, fill in a form with each distributor and ask them to submit to the IRS on your behalf to release 30% of your royalties in order for you to declare the full amount of royalties earned as income to pay taxes in your own country.

Obtaining an EIN is much easier than getting an ITIN as businesses have more priority than individuals, and being able to do it by phone is much more convenient. Before you make the call, do determine what type of corporation you are considered as in the US. There are corporate entities that exist in the US but not elsewhere, and you will be asked about this. They are not familiar with other types of corporations in other countries. If you make a mistake and register as the wrong type of corporation, you can write the IRS a letter to correct your file. Otherwise, you may be on the hook for various types of paperwork depending on the corporation you chose.

Are you feeling exhausted yet? After distributing your book around the world, you have to let people know it's there and ready for purchase. You're made a lot of sacrifices for this indie publishing venture, whether financially or sacrificing time from your personal life, so you want it to pay off. The chapter on marketing will give you some ideas on how to get the message out there!

FORMATTING AND COVER CREATION

You never get a second chance to make a first impression."

-Oscar Wilde

Before a book reaches a consumer's Kindle or Nook, or whatever e-reader they use, and before it becomes a printed product, it exists as two parts: interior and exterior files. The publishing services you choose will combine the two parts to produce the final product when it is purchased, then will deliver it to your buyers either digitally (eBook) or by mail (print book), depending on which version they purchased. Remember, eBook and print on demand publishing comes with "order fulfillment"—that means you give the publishers the files they need to fulfill, or deliver, the product to your buyers. Formatting is a design process that results in the interior file the publisher needs. Cover creation is the process of designing the cover's appearance, then creating the exterior file the publisher needs to perfect fit that design on the interior printed file and on the eBook record they deliver to the consumer.

What is Formatting?

Sometimes so much focus is given to the cover of the book that it is forgotten the design of the pages is also important. Even if a book is well written, the words have to be legible to its readers or else it won't be read! The interior design of your book's pages also impacts professional perception and enhances the reader's experience. Both will influence consumer reviews just as much as the story you've written. If a book doesn't appear to have been professionally packaged, it may not sell. If a book has design touches that enhance the visual aesthetics on the pages, the reader will enjoy it more.

Formatting involves setting up layout, margins, page numbers, running headers, indents, line spacing, paragraph spacing, font types, and font sizing. There are many decisions to make in regards to formatting, falling either under business smart choices or specifications set by the distributor's POD requirements. Business decisions could be deciding to print less pages to save money, so the font is made smaller or trim size is larger. For distributors with POD services, they usually provide a template and a guide—if they discover the file you submit doesn't meet their specifications, the file will be rejected.

You can either do the work yourself or hire someone to do it for you. Formatting is not a trivial thing and it will take some time and skill. Look up instructions and tips provided by each distributor. If you are formatting a print book, ensure you have the correct template for the trim size and page count. Images can also be a bit tricky to format, so don't be surprised if the end result doesn't work out the first time.

Deciding to publish a print book, eBook, or both is a

personal decision. Print books have more complicated formatting requirements and more cover graphics to worry about, therefore it will cost more time and money to produce. Many indie authors only offer eBooks and don't bother with print books due to these extra costs. In my experience, most of my sales come from eBooks, not print books. For this title, I wanted a print book since I speak about self-publishing at conventions and it is nice to have the actual product in hand. As well, I am not an eBook reader, so creating a print book was important to me.

If a formatter is hired, they usually guarantee the file they produce will not be rejected by a distributor. If you are doing everything yourself, I promise you there will be many late nights of reading the most mundane materials on formatting! But you will save money in the long term as you publish more products.

Book File Formats

There are different types of file formats for book publishing depending on where you want to distribute. The common file formats for publishing include Word, PDF, RTF, ePub, and Mobi. Manuscripts need to go all the way through proofreading in Word before they can be worked on in other programs for two reasons: it provides the editing tool known as Track Changes that editors and proofreaders require; and standardized formatting is done there, then the prepared content is moved to design formatting software where it is final formatted and translated to the file types you need to publish each version of your book.

- *Word (.doc, .docx)* – Microsoft product used for writing and editing your manuscript. Amazon accepts Word documents and converts them to a .mobi eBook file during the publishing process. The formatting requirements are very simple.

- *Portable Document Format (PDF)* – A file format

created by Adobe Systems that can be read by devices with Adobe Reader installed. It is usually the file type submitted for print books.

- *Rich Text Format (RTF)* – A file type created by Microsoft Corporation for compatibility with any word processor to be readable by many devices.

- *Electronic publication (ePub)* – A reflowable file type that allows readers to optimize text for a particular device. This means the consumer can adjust settings like type and size of fonts to their preferences on a variety of devices. Many eBook publishers use this format.

- *Mobipocket (Mobi)* – A reflowable file format that only works with Amazon Kindle devices or Kindle software apps, and allows the consumer to adjust settings to their preferences.

Word, PDF, and RTF files are very popular file formats easily created with a word processing program, Word being the most common. EPub and Mobi files can be created with software programs and are similar to websites with multiple files and coding. These files allow for a better reading experience because readers can customize fonts and sizing while PDF and RTF files will not allow for this. Word files can become reflowable files. When you upload a Word document to Amazon, it converts it to a Mobi file so you're actually publishing the reflowable Mobi. When you preview the eBook during your publishing steps in Amazon, it's the Mobi file you're looking at. As well, other distributors such as Smashwords and Draft2Digital can convert a Word file to ePub files.

Options for Formatting Your Manuscript

Before you start any work on formatting, decide where you want to sell your books. You will most likely need multiple file formats for the same book if you choose multiple distributors. Make note that each file format is a different version of your product, and you will need a separate ISBN number for each version. For example, one ISBN for paperback, one for hard cover, and one for eBooks. Depending on where you live, this may become costly if you are purchasing ISBNs.

Hiring someone to format your book will cost something, but is worth it if you don't have time or patience to learn how to do proper formatting. Poorly formatted works are usually not read and will leave a consumer feeling cheated.

DIY Formatting

If you do an internet search for "formatting self-publishing guides" you will find tons of free resources ranging from videos to books. Amazon has forums with discussions on formatting, so if you are using them as a distributor, you can ask questions on the forum or even contact the company. Note that Amazon offers free software, KindleGen (file conversion) and Kindle Previewer (Mobi file previewer) to help you create and test your book files. Building Your Book for Kindle is also available for free to guide you step by step through creating and uploading your files. There are authors in publishing groups on LinkedIn who dispense lots of good advice, so don't be afraid to pick their brains. The Smashwords Style Guide is available for free as well, with detailed instructions specific to their "meat grinder" program, which creates multiple eBook file formats for a variety of retailers.

For formatting work, you can either use free software or purchase something created specifically for professional formatting. If you already have Microsoft Word, you can use it for formatting some file types, although some authors have publicly stated they find it a bit difficult to use for that purpose. There are many online videos with tips to help with formatting if you decide to use this program.

Things change all the time in the world of book distribution and formatting. One good site to follow is digitalbookworld.com, which has the latest publishing industry news and educational resources.

Examples of free software for formatting:

- *Calibre* (calibre-ebook.com) – has limited functions compared to other software, such as lack of templates, but is good for basic formatting.

- *iBooks Author* (apple.com/ca/ibooks-author) – allows you to add sound and video into eBooks and can translate work into different languages, but you need to have an Apple computer to use this software.

Examples of software you can purchase:

- *Scrivener* (literatureandlatte.com/scrivener.php) – this is also a writing software, which can organize book chapters, plot lines, and research ideas, and you can use it for eBook formatting. Note that the Scrivener Windows version is less functional than the Scrivener Mac version.

- *Jutoh* (jutoh.com) – includes a built in cover designer and can import existing content for editing.

- *Creatavist* (creatavist.com) - can do magazine formatting and translate your work into different languages.

- *InDesign* (adobe.com) – a very powerful Adobe tool with a steep learning curve; used by professionals in the industry.

Hiring a Formatter

The price of formatting a book depends on the word count, pages, heading divisions (chapters and extra pages), complex elements like bullet point sections, and amount of images in the manuscript. Some formatters will not quote a price unless they see the manuscript first so they can calculate how much work they have to do. I have dealt with formatters who can handle both eBooks and print books, as well as those who only create eBooks.

Similar to hiring an editor, have a few questions on hand before committing. A few suggested questions:

- How many books have you formatted?

- Do you format graphics? (if needed)

- Do you format print books and eBooks? What file types do you offer?

- Do you guarantee your formatting work? After formatting, do you allow a proofing run with my distributor and guarantee you'll correct any issues that prevent my file from being accepted? (The formatter I work with allows up to 30 corrections post first format.)

- After publishing, if mistakes are found, how much for corrections?

The cheapest quotes I have found are on Fiverr.com for eBook conversions, starting at about $5 for fifteen pages. Read the reviews of previous customers before committing to anything as sometimes cheap does not mean reliable or good service. Other freelance websites (reedsy.com, upwork.com, and freelancer.com) also have people offering their services. Since print is more complicated to format, it will cost more than eBook formatting. Usually if you commit to both eBook and print formatting from one source, you should be able to get a discount.

Smashwords has a list of people they recommend and Amazon can help you with formatting for a fee (they hire free lancers to do the work). Generally, if you hire someone, it's better to hire directly because there isn't an extra layer there in case you need to contact them again for changes.

Post Formatting Checks

Uploading a manuscript to a distributor site takes only a few minutes and the eBook will be available for sale within hours. This speed is a little bit frightening considering an author may have slaved over the manuscript for years! For print books, you should order a "proof" copy to ensure that its quality meets your standards before putting it up for sale. The book will be sent via snail mail, and there may be a small customs fee if you don't live in the same country as the distributor.

After formatting is complete, be sure to check for a few things prior to uploading your book. These are just suggestions and each distributor will have their own guidelines as well.

- *Be careful with page numbers* - Page numbers help the readers navigate through the book, however, some pages shouldn't have them, such as copyright and title page. The front matter can be numbered using small Roman numerals, then the first page of the story or main body begins with page one. Page one is an odd numbered page and should be on the right. Even numbered pages are on the left. If the story is broken into multiple parts such as Part 1, Part 2, etc., then the title page for the section may be included in the numbering count, but not shown on the page.

- *No headers on blank pages* - If there are blank pages,

they should have no text. Blank pages can fall on either left or right hand facing pages to cause other pages to fall a certain way.

- *Capitalizing items properly* - Titles, subtitles, chapter titles, and subheads should all be capitalized or title case capitalized.

- *One space between sentences* - Don't double space between sentences, or if you do by habit, replace them with single spaces during editing.

- *Justify the text* - The book should be fully justified, which means the text on the page should appear rectangular with text lines expanding from the left margin all the way to the right margin.

- *Adequate margin spacing* - Don't try to cram words onto fewer pages to save on printing costs! Leave enough space in the gutter (area where pages are bound) and around the perimeter of the text so readers feel comfortable when reading the book.

- *EBook page numbers depend on the file type* - Non-reflowable formats such as PDFs have pages numbered the same way as print books and may be inaccurate on the consumer's reader since their screen size can vary. Reflowable formats such as ePub and Mobi files can display page numbers, controlled by the consumer. Formatting can make it possible for these to generate page numbers on their readers, but consumers may turn that off on their technology. Page numbers have little value in e-reading technology as their device usually gives location information instead.

Generally, there is a lot more to worry about with a print book versus an eBook. EBooks contain only one screen page, so you only have to worry about margins along the outside of the text. If the formatting is done incorrectly for eBooks, uploading another version can be done quickly. If something screws up with a print book, it will take awhile to fix because you won't know if your corrections made a difference until the next print run.

A physical book consists of pages bound together. When you open up a book, you are looking at two pages, or a spread. The middle of the book is called a gutter and requires wider margins to allow room for the binding. If the margins are too close to the gutter, the text will be cut off. Too small or too large of a margin will affect the overall readability of the book and the result won't look professional. Around the margins is the "bleed" space, which is an area beyond the border for printing. If text is within the bleed space, words will be cut off.

A common formatting issue for both print and eBooks is interior images. Unless they are crucial to the book, it may be a good idea to steer clear of images as much as possible. They could be tricky to translate into file formats correctly. One formatter I spoke with really discouraged images. Over time, as you perfect your formatting skills or hire an experienced formatter, this would not be an issue. If you are including images in your book, keep in mind you will need at least 300DPI for print books. EBooks can be published with images of lower DPI. Using the same image for print and eBooks is fine as long as it's at least 300DPI.

After reading through a newly published eBook or print book, you may still find mistakes. To correct this, you will have to fix all the mistakes yourself or pay the formatter to do it for you. Then all the files have to be uploaded again to the distribution site. If the site distributes to multiple retailers, there may be a lag in the update appearing everywhere due to the involvement of so many parties. If desired, you can release it as a new edition or note on the copyright page which version you uploaded to avoid any confusion.

What is Cover Design?

The second most crucial item to a book is a great cover. This visual item will either draw people towards your book or make them run in the opposite direction. Covers are very subjective and there is no right or wrong answer as to what different people like or don't like. You are making a first impression with the cover and sadly, looks do matter.

Remember that your cover also represents your workmanship as a publishing professional, so if you want to be seen as a competent author, an excellent cover will help build your reputation. I have seen covers created from no more than stock art thrown onto a blank digital canvas, which made me not want to read the book. Since it didn't seem like anyone spent much time on the cover, it made me question if anyone spent time editing.

The cover should give some clues as to what the book is about and should be intriguing enough to catch a reader's eye. A striking image, bold color, special effect, and nice font styles are all things that make consumers pause long enough to read your title. Font is as important as art and they should work together in harmony. Having a silly font on a serious drama book can kill its mood and artwork. Keep in mind that most people will see the thumbnail of your cover first, so make sure the title and author name is legible in that smaller view.

According to Digital Book World and Writer's Digest 2014 author survey, books with contracted professional cover art generated more income than those that did not. Of authors that made no income, only 22% had contracted with a professional cover art designer; of authors making more than $5,000, 52% had contracted art; and of those earning over $25,000, 64% had contracted art. From Para Publishing's author survey, indie authors indicated they paid an average of $276 for an illustration, $3,500 for a complex cover design, and the price range was $450-$3,000 for a cover design.

Similar to manuscript copy blindness, if you are going to make your own cover, ask around for honest opinions before committing. Your cover will not only be used for the book, it will be the main image for all book marketing materials such as website, bookmarks, and business cards.

Take the time to look at published titles in your genre at the library or bookstores for inspiration. You will discover many ideas that will help you with your cover. Consider colors, fonts, types of illustrations, and other details to make your cover stand out from all these books. Don't be afraid to mix and match elements you like from different books. Doing some research is important because even if you hire a professional to help you with the cover, you will want to ensure your book design is comparable with others in your genre. The professionals you hire should have more knowledge than you on such things, and should bring marketing expertise to the table, so take their advice for good design.

Elements of a Print Book Cover and eBook Cover

A cover for a print book has three components: the front, the spine, and the back. An eBook only has the front cover and no spine or back. The most important piece of real estate for a print book cover is the spine since most people store books with the spine facing outward. For eBooks, the only item you have to worry about is the front cover.

Before starting work on any covers, take a hard look into what it takes to make a professional cover in terms of tools and skills. At this point, determine if leaving the design and file creation work up to the experts will be in the best interest of your project long term.

Most distributors have their own template to ensure covers are printed properly on their machines. For a print book, the cover file is the last thing you create because the number of pages will affect the width of the spine, which in turn affects placement of content over artwork on both the front and back cover. If you are just doing an eBook and you know what you want on the cover, you can make it anytime as it is not dependent on the size of the interior like the jacket wrap of a print book is.

Typically, print covers need a higher resolution of at least 300DPI and you have to know your page count, paper selection, and trim size of the book to generate the template. For eBooks, the resolution of 75DPI is usually enough, but if you want to create promotional items such as banners, you may want a file of higher resolution to prevent blurriness when printing.

An understanding of the rules of licensing levels for stock images, how colors impact buyer behavior, using color settings to preserve image quality at print, and experience with creative design and marketing is preferable for the best possible cover.

Front Cover

The front cover frequently contains a visual image, which can be either stock art or a commissioned illustration, along with book title, author name, and book number if it is part of a series. Looking at published titles, you will notice books aimed at female audiences tend to have more flourishing details such as flowers and swirly lines, while books aimed at men feature straight lines and dark colors. Romance books have handsome men or luscious looking maidens and erotica books feature something even sexier. Fantasy and science fiction books tend to have very complicated covers with creative illustrations. By looking at books in your genre, you will be able to figure out what style of cover could best attract your target audience. Sometimes book critic blurbs are placed on the cover, but these words could also be placed on the back cover or front pages of the book.

Spine

For the spine of a print book, the title and name of the author should be clearly stated and graphics should be kept at a minimum to prevent overcrowding. The fonts of the text should match the front of the book for consistency. It's important that the title and author name can be read clearly since this is how a reader will find the book on their shelves.

If part of a series, each book should have the same style of fonts and graphic elements in order to match up on the shelf. Another thing to remember is that edges of the spine will be wrapped onto the book, so be weary of the spine borders or the graphics will bleed onto the front or the back cover. The cover template from the distributor will let you know how much space you have for the spine and where the border lines fall.

If you have incorporated a publishing company, consider having a professional logo made and displaying it on the bottom part of the spine. This little detail can make your book compare better with other traditionally published books when placed next to them on a book shelf.

Back Cover

The most important part of the back of a print book is a clearly displayed synopsis or book blurb in a clean, legible font. The purpose of the blurb is to compel readers to want to read the book, so the text must be concise and intriguing.

A few pointers to help you get started on the blurb:

- It should be short and simple with a length of

about 100-150 words.

- Present an interesting idea about the plot and protagonist (name the main character) for fiction books or let the reader know what problem they could solve by reading your nonfiction book. However, do not give away the story and leave some mystery to intrigue the reader.

- Set the mood of the story to let readers know if the book is serious or comedic.

- Stay true to your genre by reading other blurbs to make sure you will meet your prospective reader's expectations.

- Practice writing the blurb—write one and rewrite again. The shorter it is, the harder it is to write.

The blurb will be used for marketing materials such as PR packages and on websites, so do spend some time crafting a compelling message as to why someone would be interested in your book. There are many tips available online on how to write these, along with examples, so take the time to do a quick search and gather some ideas.

Some back covers have wrap around graphics or blocks of color to make things more creatively interesting. Obviously, the colors and elements should match the front. The distributor cover template will also include a space for an International Standard Book Number (ISBN) barcode image.

After uploading the cover for a print book, order a proof copy to make sure your finished product prints correctly. Sometimes what you see on the screen is not exactly what is printed. Things will never print perfectly to match the digital display on your computer, so remember to leave a bit of extra space between front, spine, and back cover margins in case of any shifts.

I printed about ten proof copies for *The Undead Sorceress* (my first novel). Every copy printed differently and there were tiny shifts in the spine image. Around the same time, I met with a small bookstore owner to talk about consignment selling. After listening to me lament about my proof issues, he sighed and said I was obsessing too much. "Every book will never be perfect in your eyes, but they look fine to me and everyone else," he assured. This taught me not to obsess too much over minor details for the cover and to be satisfied with the macro details. As long as the major elements of the cover are visible and the interior print is clean (no blobs of ink in the book), the shift of a 0.25mm line on the spine due to printing alignment won't really matter.

Different Options for Cover Creation

There are a number of options available for creating a cover, ranging from doing it yourself to buying a readymade cover. Which route you take depends on what skills you have and how complicated you envision you book cover will be.

- *Do It Yourself (DIY) cover from scratch or build on distributor site* – If you are creating the cover yourself, you can use graphics software to combine graphics and fonts together. Alternatively, a few distributor sites such as Amazon have online cover designer software with stock art and fonts pre-loaded so you can just design a cover directly on their site.

- *A custom cover made by a cover designer and an artist* – A cover designer is the person who creates the cover and an artist provides the illustration. If you do not require a custom illustration, cover designers can make a cover with stock art.

- *Buying a pre-made cover* – There are sites available on the internet for you to buy readymade covers.

The DIY Cover

If you are going to make the cover yourself, you will need a computer with some basic graphic software. There are many graphic software choices available on the market with the golden standards being Adobe Illustrator and Adobe Photoshop. There is a steep learning curve for these softwares, but they are fantastic tools. If you are working with a limited budget, the best free software available, in my opinion, is paint.net. Paint.net is truly free software that is not a trial version or a program that will add watermarks of their logo to everything you create. If you want to contribute to this software, their website getpaint.net will accept donations. However, bear in mind, there are limitations to free software, so it may not be able to do everything your heart desires.

Attractive graphics are imperative to a good cover. When searching for images, look for royalty free ones. Why is this important? Because it means you don't have to share some of your book royalties with the artist who created the image. Does this mean they are crappy quality graphics? No, some of them are superb! The artists who give away their work want to be hired eventually, similarly to indie authors who give out their books wanting to be published traditionally one day. Everyone is aware they need to get their stuff out into the world in hopes of a future opportunity.

When a search is conducted for free graphics, there are always nicer images displayed in parallel that are available for purchase. Usually it's a good idea to download the highest graphic resolution possible, especially if you are creating a print cover. Prior to using any images, do read the license terms. Some sites will allow you to copy, modify, and distribute even for commercial purposes, without asking permission and without paying attribution. Other sites will have a specific clause limiting the number of books you can sell with the graphic.

Some wonderful sites where you can find royalty free graphics include: pixabay.com, freeimages.com, and istockphoto.com.

Fonts deserve a lot more credit than what they are given. They communicate if the book is whimsical or serious, setting the tone for the reader.

Your computer's operating system software will come with a good selection of fonts, but if you want a specific one, you will have to search for it. Similar to images, some are free for use while others require a fee for commercial use. To use these fonts after downloading, you have to unzip the files with a program such as 7zip, then save them into your computer's font folder. Look up instructions from font websites to locate your specific operating system's folder and, after saving the files properly, you will be able to use the font style in any program on your computer.

A few good font sites with clear license terms are dafont.com, fontsquirrel.com, 1001freefonts.com, and fontmaster.com.

The back cover panel for a print book has an ISBN barcode image, which needs to be created. The barcode is an image that can be scanned to look up the book's information, which is the record you control if you own the ISBN. One site that can help you generate this graphic for free is bookow.com. Usually the distributor will indicate where the bar code should be placed on their print cover templates.

When you are done with the cover, be sure to test it. Send it to a few people and ask for their first impressions.

The feedback will help you improve the cover if you look for friends and family who will be honest with you and not worry about hurting your feelings. If you are eventually going to sell your book to strangers, you need to be ready for how an unbiased consumer will respond to your cover—they will write reviews with no concern for your feelings!

The DIY Cover From a Distributor Site

As mentioned before, some distributor sites like Amazon have an online cover design program with fonts and stock art pre-loaded so you can create a cover on their site. This is something I've never tried because I didn't find their available selection of stock art desirable for my project. The program is limited, so don't expect to do fancy stuff like layering or special effects.

The convenience factor is high for this option as you don't have to install any special software or hunt for graphics. As well, you don't have to worry about fitting your cover graphic onto any template because that will be done automatically by their program. There is a chance that someone else may have created a similar cover because the stock art is not plentiful or unique.

If you are pressed for time, this is the fastest route. After creating the cover, you can save the image while in the preview mode and get an actual size jpeg file that may be usable for some marketing materials. If you want to make t-shirts or banners, you should check if the file resolution is good enough and if the license will allow you to use the image for such marketing purposes.

The Custom Cover

Professional cover designers and artists are hired for

custom covers, and work as freelancers or in design teams. The cover designer is trained to design your cover concept and create the file types to perfectly fit all of your publishing versions. These designers are often also artists, work in partnership with artists, and/or know artists who can create the huge range of art types a client may want. For a custom image, artists can craft a digital illustration or paint/draw an original art piece to your specifications. If the scope of your artwork is beyond the cover designer's abilities, or the abilities of artists in their team, they may refer you out to find a freelance artist who does nothing but create art work for many purposes, including books. Shopping this depends on your budget and your vision for the cover. If you decide stock art is sufficient, your cost will be much less than if you commission original art work.

For my non-fiction books, I prefer stock art that is clean like the writing in the book, simple, and to the point. For my fantasy works, I prefer more artistic, original art work to bring my imaginary world to life. It is all a matter of personal preference. If you work with a cover designer with experience creating covers in your genre, trust their instincts and design.

The Cover Designer:

If you have some graphic art skills, you may wonder why you would want to hire a cover designer. Cover design also requires the ability to take an illustration or stock art, combine it with design, fonts, color, special graphic effects, and make something super fantastic. There is a method to this madness. Although I see a clear cover image in my head, after a professional designer's polishing touches and additional design ideas, books always look and perform better. They are like an editor for the cover and bring marketing and consumer behavior experience to the table.

The Steps to Commissioning a Cover:

1) *Think about what you want to commission* – It's

important that you spend time developing your vision and not change your mind midway through the design process. If you are not clear on what you want, believe me, the designer will have a hard time delivering the goods to your standards. Delays can occur that cost time and significant changes can be costly.

2) *Create a Spec* – You know what you want, but now you have to communicate it to someone else. Try to provide as many details as possible. I won't lie to you, writing a creative brief or spec document is a lot of work. You are translating a visual image from your head for someone to recreate just as you imagined. Search the internet for similar pictures, pantone colors, and styles of drawings to help the designer understand your vision.

If the designer doesn't read your specs, it will be apparent when they deliver your cover! It helps to include the following:

- Cover styles you want (send them covers of what you like)

- A description and example of images

- What colors you prefer

- Fonts you want for your name, title, subtitle, or back description

- Special elements or images for the spine, front, and back covers

- Preference to where the ISBN graphic is placed

- Distributor's cover template and requirements document

- Request for original file and file types you

want (pdf, jpeg, etc.)

- Ask if you can purchase the "working" files, so you can edit in the future. This may not be possible in some cases due to their licensing agreement with the software company and/or font packages they use to create your publishing files. For future editing, you will need compatible software if you can get the working files or you can go back to that designer. Designers normally keep archived files for all clients as making changes after publishing is not uncommon.

3) *Search for a cover designer* – You can choose between freelancers easily found with search engine keywords "freelance cover designer" or websites that facilitate project bidding. There are many websites available that specialize in connecting freelancers with authors, including reedsy.com, bibliocrunch.com, freelancer.com, fiverr.com or upwork.com.

99designs.com has all sorts of graphic designers to bid on jobs. You upload the specs for what you want and people send you images of the cover they have designed. There could potentially be hundreds of different designs to choose from. Crowd source comments can be solicited to help you choose which cover you want. You only pay for one cover in the end and the site has basic packages starting at $299.

4) *Look through their portfolios* – Each cover designer has a different style, so going through their collection will help you decide if you like their work or not. Designers tend to specialize in specific genres, so finding the right match starts with seeing if they usually create the type of cover you're looking for.

5) *Make contact* – If buying the service from a site, you may have to fill in a form or you can email the person directly with the specs. Also check if they will supply stock art or expect you to send them art. The designer will send you a quote based on all of these things. If you go through a third party (website service such as fiverr.com), usually there is some sort of guarantee so you can get your money back if something goes wrong. Otherwise, use PayPal as the form of payment since they provide a buyer protection guarantee.

6) *Evaluate options* – Each person will quote you different prices. To help with making the decision, go through their portfolios once again.

7) *Make a deal* – You can ask if it is possible to pay in installments if working with someone new. Always remember to establish a due date schedule for first drafts, also known as galleys, and for project completion date. Then send out sorry notes to the unsuccessful candidates. It's only decent to let other people know you hired someone else.

8) *Finalizing the Cover* – The designer should send you some galleys to note any design changes before the various file types are created. Usually you can ask for at least one to two changes before committing. Ask if the stock art used was royalty free just to have this on record in case of any disputes in regards to the graphic used. If you provided your own illustration, you should own the copyright or have permission to use it.

I've hired cover designers and also designed some covers myself. For one book, the cover designer said my specs were too complicated (a few special effect requests) and he wanted to raise the price to something I couldn't afford. I had a choice of making things more simple or completing it myself. Since I have some graphic software experience, I decided to finish the cover myself, although it took a bit longer and affected my schedule. Another cover was a stock art cover with a relatively simple concept and no special effect requests, so I had no trouble hiring someone to help me with this job.

You will use the book cover image over and over again, so make sure the fonts are clear even if the image is very small—in thumbnail view like is shown in book lists on Amazon especially. When people click on your book's sale page, they see the thumbnail image of your cover. You're depending on them to see something they like, then buy your book!

The Artist

An artist is a special someone you hire to create a piece of custom art for you. Similar to hiring a cover designer, you will have to give specific instructions in order to ensure your vision is properly translated into the work. Do remember to ask for a copyright transfer be included in the contract, so you are not bound to let the artist know and perhaps pay a fee every time you use the image. Usually the artist will ask for a copyright transfer fee, which is a onetime payment and you should maintain the original of the signed agreement for the life of the product using that image.

When you work with the artist you want to set a book publishing timeline to include some extra days in case lateness occurs. Some artists are great at delivery on time and others not so much. The timing for art delivery varies depending on the artist. The cost of a piece of artwork can range from $0 to $3000. This difference is due to many things, ranging from the country they live in to professional illustration experience. Don't be afraid to ask to pay for the work in installments as sometimes you need to do this in order to keep the work on schedule.

The Steps to Commissioning Artwork:

1) *Think about what you want to commission* – Are there certain characters from your book you want to have illustrated or a certain scene? Think about the mood you want to evoke from your future reader when they look at this piece of art.

2) *Write down the specs* – Artists cannot read minds. You will have to be very clear about what you want them to create. Search for similar examples of illustration styles, decide on a color palette, and gather references such as faces, clothing, and poses to show them your vision.

   It helps to include the following:

   • Intro sentence about what the art is about and what it is for

   • Do you want to own the copyright for future reproduction or is this a one-off that will never be reproduced? Usually the artist retains all copyrights unless you ask for it to be transferred for a price (cost depends on artist).

   • The style you want – Realistic? Manga? Cartoon?

   • Find some references of stuff you like. The idea is to let the artist know what kind of style, color palette, and "feeling" you want to invoke from the art.

   • Describe each character, if any. How old are they? Height? Facial features, clothing, as if they are real people to the artist.

   • Find specific references for things such as poses, fashion style, faces, etc. for any character images

- What is in the background? Do you want nothing (plain color) or a specific environment (forest, for example)?

Lastly, don't freak out if the first piece isn't what you imagined—it may take a few tries before the artist can draw what you had in mind! The artists I've worked with will send a few line sketches to make sure the outlines and details are fine before they start coloring. It is much more difficult to change things after many layers of colors and special effects have been applied.

3) *Search for an artist* – They are listed at some of the same websites as cover designers: deviantart.com, redbubble.com, upwork.com, fiverr.com, freelancer.com and 99designs.com.

4) *Look through their portfolios* – It is not fun looking for artists as you will be overwhelmed by the different styles and prices available. A person may be super cheap at $5 for a piece of art, but can they deliver your vision? Another person's art looks fantastic, but they want $1200. Can you afford this?

You may have a picture or style in mind already, but you have to search hard for the right people to make your dream come true. Don't settle for something your gut tells you is not right. This is not very scientific advice, I'm afraid, but following your instincts is super important!

5) *Make contact* – You may email the artist directly or go through a third party website such as 99designs.com. Sometimes you may get a better deal if you pay the artist directly as you can negotiate on the price. There is always a bit

of risk with dealing with a new person, but usually if the artist has a decent website and looks legit, I would take this risk to save some money.

Commissioned art can range from $0 (bartering for future favors) to $3000 USD in my experience. Sometimes the price varies depending on how many people are drawn in each piece of art or if you want a nice background.

6) *Evaluate options* – Each artist will quote you different prices, so look at their portfolios again to compare styles.

7) *Make the deal* – You can ask if it is possible to pay in installments and always establish a due date for the art. Then send out sorry notes to the unsuccessful candidates. It's only decent to let other people know that you hired someone else.

8) *Finalizing the Artwork* – Usually the artist will send you some drafts to make note of any changes. There should be some back and forth before the art is finalized. For artists that don't earn much or if you drive them crazy, they will sometimes ask for more money per change. But usually you can ask for at least one to two changes before the work is completed.

9) *Copyright transfer* – This should be discussed when making the deal and always send a contract for them to sign for copyright transfer after the work is complete. Include a jpeg thumbnail of the art you commissioned, inserted in the contract so it's part of the record. For personal artwork, this is usually not done as it is typically not reproduced for sale.

Most artists will charge you a fee for transferring copyright and the price can vary. You also have a choice about letting them keep a copy of the artwork in their portfolio to show others in the future, which could result in exposure for your product too. Ask the artist to display it with a link to your book's sale page and/or website in their online portfolio and send them some business cards for any studio displays.

After you have this great piece of artwork, you can use it for your cover and manipulate the graphic for all your marketing needs. You might want to add a watermark or a copyright logo (if you have the copyright on the art) and your name to indicate it's yours in some applications. When used for social media memes, banners, and posts, add your website for people who want to look up where the art came.

The Pre-Made Cover

Creating a custom cover is a lot of work, especially when you have to hire multiple parties to help you finish it. There are online companies who sell pre-made stock art covers. All you have to do after purchasing the cover file is type in your name and title of the book. This is probably the most painless option out of all the cover creation methods since all the work is already done.

Where to Find a Pre-Made Cover

Do a search online for "pre made covers" and you will find many companies offering cover products for purchase. Sometimes there are sales on covers not selling as quickly, so you can pick one up for as little as $30.

Note that most companies only sell eBook covers, not print covers. Remember to check the DPI if you want to use this cover for future marketing materials. As well, ask if the cover is one of a kind or not and if there are any limitations like how many downloads are allowed.

Similar to a well wrapped present, a beautiful cover speaks volumes about the quality of the contents. Creating a cover is one of the most fun things you will do while creating your indie book. Spend some time perfecting the first and last thing people may remember!

THE MARKETING BLACK HOLE

---

*"Money coming in says I've made
the right marketing decisions."*

-Adam Osborne

In order to gain new readers, you have to tell the world about your work. If you had a traditional publisher, their marketing department would help spread the news, but you will want to market also, and often are required to as part of the contract. A publisher's marketing budget is most likely reserved for famous authors who have proven they can earn a large return on investment for the company with minimal risk.

Since you are on your own, you will have to do the marketing work yourself. It's not as scary as it sounds and you can spend as much or as little as you want. It is a black hole because you can spend money indefinitely—marketing never ends. There are services available to help you, of course, but overall, you will need to form a vision about where to focus your marketing efforts that is right for your product, the business of being an author, and your budget.

Why is Marketing Needed?

The goal of marketing is to successfully introduce your book to the right people at the right time. If you can do this, you will gain both sales for your book and a loyal audience to help you spread the word about all of your work. Good "word-of-mouth" is the best advertising for any book and writing career.

Marketing is about letting people know you can fulfill their need. Someone once told me that an author is like a hot dog vendor on every street corner a consumer encounters and you must get in their faces and make them see you. They will hurry right past you to buy books from another author who has made sure they've got the market's attention. You don't have to be an aggressive person, but you do need to work at selling your goods and interact with consumers. Marketing is much more social and technology based these days, and matching your marketing to your sales plan is important. If you're primarily depending on internet based retail sources like Amazon, your marketing is more likely to reach those consumers by being internet/online based. From social media to pay per click advertising and boosted ad copy, you can grow internet followings and social networks. Please do not become one of those authors that only sends out "buy my book" ad copy over and over again. This is annoying and does not work with the more social influenced consumer behaviors of today!

Questions to Think About

To help form a vision of what type of marketing you want to do, below are a few questions to help you outline your overall project. In the appendix, I have included a basic budget sheet to help you with the finance part of publishing, and how much you have for marketing is what's left after what you have already spent on production out of your total budget.

Marketing can quickly break your book budget as it is a black hole for money. Keep in mind that it will always be difficult to measure eyeballs and not all tactics will generate a sale. Even if you are financing this personally, you have to ask yourself: How will you ensure any return on your investment?

Add or delete points to consider depending on what fits your project. There are no rules—this is your planning exercise, do what you feel best!

Overview of book

- Name of book
- Synopsis
- Two genre categories it fits into

Who do you want to sell to?

- Target audience is how old, where do they live?
- How does your target market buy books?
- What popular culture trends do they follow?

What are the trends in the book industry?

- What type of book formats are popular?
- What distributors and retailers will work best for your books?
- Any upcoming predictions for books in your genre category?

What's your competitor doing?

- Distribution channels

- average price of books
- length of books
- successful marketing strategies
- unsuccessful marketing strategies

What do you need to complete and package this book? (Budget building)

- Editing
- Artist for concept art
- Cover designer
- Formatter
- Printing costs
- ISBN and copyright costs

What type of marketing do you want to invest in?

- Build an author webpage or website
- Create author profile pages
- Book reviews
- Social media
- Free and/or discounting promotions
- Elevator Pitch
- Consignment book selling
- Making promo stuff
- Press releases and press kit
- Create a book trailer
- Competitions
- Advertising: radio, television, print, internet
- Online book tours

- Cover and book trailer reveals

- Book launch event

- Donate your book

- Guest speaking: libraries, schools, book clubs, book stores, conventions

Action plan and timelines

- If you have a set goal of when you want your book launch, work backwards

- If you want to do pre-release marketing, set your publishing date around the time needed for your marketing efforts

Financial stuff

- Define your budget.

- Create a backup plan for if you go over budget.

- Determine your business structure and how you will handle taxes

The Author Platform

An author platform is the stage an author stands on to put their brand and products in front of consumers. The term refers to all of the pieces that create a public presence, whether online or offline, or both, where the author showcases their reputation, products, successes, and failures to readers and other professionals in the publishing industry. It is not something that can come into existence overnight, but rather, takes time to build.

The platform is defined differently by different people, but it generally consists of your work, social media profiles and influence ranking, quantitative evidence such as website traffic, qualitative evidence such as book reviews and loyal readers, and a website and/or blog. It's not about hard selling your books at all, but rather you as the author being able to consistently produce quality work. There is a fine line between being authentic and pushing yourself outside your comfort zone, which will make you appear phony.

Building a platform could begin by publishing your book first, then building a website to promote it. Then create your Amazon, Goodreads, or other author profile pages to get a start in the book community. Join social media outlets to discuss topics related to your book or share your struggles with other authors. By doing some of these things, you are laying down the foundation for future opportunities to further your career as a writer.

You may think this platform building sounds like acting, and in a way it is. In life, you play many roles from daughter/son to work colleague, and now that of an author and business person if you are going to self-publish. Readers and fans are strangers who will expect a certain authority and personality from you. For example, comedians are expected to be very funny people offstage; however, many of them are quite serious in real life. It takes a lot of work and effort to write jokes and manage the business of their work. If you demonstrate confidence in yourself, people will trust that your work is just as good as how you appear. The style of your platform may also have a lot to do with your target audience. If your audience is religious, you would have a positive, family oriented appearance with no bad language in social media feeds and connections. Alternatively, if your audience is interested in living a healthy lifestyle, on your blog you may want to post healthy recipes that taste good.

Social Media

Recognize that social media is just people communicating with one another on computers and media devices. Instead of speaking, people are texting, messaging, or posting. If you have ever participated on popular websites or apps, you know that you can talk to lots of people, simultaneously, from all around the world. Social based networking can be more effective than old fashioned advertising, at least until you are well-known and your brand inspires buying behaviors.

There are many different social media platforms and any one of them can take up a lot of time. Depending on the time you are able to devote to this type of marketing, you may want to use none, some, or all. Like all relationships, you have to start small and build trust and rapport with the audience. You have to be there with an eye catching profile; remember to answer any questions in a timely manner; and use a variety of messaging that shows you have more depth than just trying to sell a book.

The social media tools popular today may be history tomorrow. To decide what tool you want to use, pick one with software you are comfortable using from the most popular, widely used networks when you are ready. Be sure to look for programs that aggregate your messaging. Instead of logging into three different social media accounts to post messages individually, you can use a software program with a dashboard that lets you post the same message on all the different social media accounts at once. You can also set when your messages are to be published, allowing you to automate daily messaging to keep your audience listening. One such tool, available for free with their company name on your posts, or for a monthly subscription fee without telltale branding, is Hootsuite. You can write one message or upload lists of scheduled messages and simultaneously post to Twitter, Facebook, Instagram, Google+, LinkedIn, and WordPress.

Always remember that after you launch public profiles

and messaging campaigns that brand you as an author, you will always be watched. The internet is not a forgiving place if you manage to offend the wrong people. You may do ten things right, but if you mess up the eleventh thing, that may be all you will be remembered for. Social medial is a double edged sword; it can either help you cut through the weeds to find your audience, or it might lead to your demise with an audience throwing virtual rocks at you. Do be careful!

Marketing Ideas

All marketing efforts will cost you time and/or money, so choose wisely. There are many tried and true methods available, and listed below are some for you to think about.

What works for one author may not work for another. No matter what idea you choose to go with, remember to have fun as you will end up connecting with lots of different people and gain lots of experiences you never imagined!

1. Build an Author Webpage or Website

Prepare for people to run a search online for your name. If nothing comes up, the authenticity of you as an author will be questioned.

There are many free and easy ways to have a basic online presence. Register for a Google account and open a blogger.com webpage. It doesn't cost anything and you can start building something from there with their free template designer and attractive backgrounds. Over time as you feel more comfortable, you can invest in buying your own domain name and use Wordpress to build a basic website. Wordpress has a free option, or an $18 a year option that allows you to own your domain name. Don't worry if things are not perfect the first time, because you can always take down and rebuild your webpage or website. Do update it once in awhile so people know you are alive—static, unmaintained pages are less appealing and have less chance of growing into decent SEO rankings.

2. Create Author Profile Pages

Retailer sites such as Amazon and Kobo have author page profiles you can fill in. On your book's sales page there will be a link to your profile page consumers can click to learn more about you and access all the books you have for sale. Goodreads is another site where you can build an author page and also share what books you have been reading lately to the book community.

3. Book Reviews

This is one of the most important marketing tools for a book. Readers do read reviews before deciding if they want to purchase a book so it's essential that you have them. There are many book review sites you can write to request a review. Some are free and some are paid. It's up to you if you think it's worth spending money to pay for a review, but always remember that sometimes you might not like the results. This can be time consuming and take a great deal of time to see results from.

Ask your family and friends who have read your book to post a review, though this will be difficult and may feel like pulling teeth as you may find family and friends would rather be doing something else! Some relatives have told me that they would not read my book even if I paid them because they are not readers. Don't assume everyone you know wants to read, but you don't lose anything by asking.

Don't pay someone to post reviews onto retail pages that you wrote for your own book. This is just lazy and dishonest. It is also embarrassing if anyone ever finds out, and consumers can usually see right through such tactics. You do not want to be ridiculed by internet trolls for doing this. There will no doubt be bad reviews as well, but all reviews are good advertising and even if bad, still might entice someone to buy your book.

4. Ask for Social Media Help

You can ask your family, friends, and readers to post their review or recommend your book on their social media page. There is nothing like word of mouth to help you sell more books. If someone doesn't have time or want to do it, don't bug them or you might get the opposite effect you were hoping for.

5. Free or Discount Price Promotion

There are mixed opinions about giving books away. One of my editors did not agree with this tactic. "Your work is worth something; if you give it out, no one needs to buy the book." However, some authors use these promotion strategies if they have a series of books or may just be starting out and need the exposure. Usually they give out the first book and expect people to pay for the sequel. The freebie allows readers to see if they like an author's writing style, encouraging them to come back for more books later.

Keep in mind there are thousands of free books available. Even at the price of $0, you are still just one in a herd of many. Just because it's free doesn't mean you will automatically gain an audience. You still need other marketing in place or else people won't notice your book.

Many author websites or retail book pages allow a preview of books. If people like the sneak peek, they will want more. Both getting people to read a sample of your work from a preview at full price or giving away a free book will require marketing efforts to bring attention to the offering. The preview is based on the length of the book. The longer the book, the more preview pages made available to the consumer. If you decide to publish short stories, which can be less than twenty pages, you may wish to not include a lot of front matter or else the preview may not show any text beyond the copyright page.

Discounting refers to giving out coupons or having a sale. On certain distribution channels such as Smashwords, you can generate coupon codes for dollars off, percentage off, or free and also set an expiration date. You can choose to put a limit on how many coupons can be redeemed to control things a bit in case your discount code goes viral.

Amazon Kindle will let you do a limited time free book promotion (if you sign up for their KDP select program) and when the promotion is over, people will have to pay for your book. This can be instrumental in rising up the rankings quickly. Of course, it's expected that the book ranking will drop again once it's not free, but you have gained a chance to get some reviews and let people know the book ranked very well at one point.

6. Write Your Elevator Pitch

This is a summary of your book in two or three sentences. When you meet people and tell them you have written a book, you will naturally be asked, "What is your book about?" You have their attention for ten seconds, so practice answering this question. Over time you will get used to telling what your book is about over and over again.

7. Consignment Book Selling

As mentioned in the first chapter, you can talk to small independent book store owners to ask if they will stock your book on a consignment basis. It's a good idea to have a signed contract in regards to how the profit will be split and an agreement of how many copies you will provide. Many bookstores will not accept CreateSpace printed books, so check on this if you it's part of your plan before choosing your POD distributor.

8. Making Promo Materials

A common promo item is a bookmark matching your book cover. If you know how to use a graphics program, it's relatively simple to create. Alternatively, some online printers have web based programs with free art and text you can use to make a bookmark after you upload your book cover image.

There are endless promo materials you can create, but be careful about spending too much as you get caught up in the excitement of a book release. Each item doesn't cost too much, but printing in quantity does add up. You can make business cards, notebooks, t-shirts, mugs, caps, tote bags, pens, etc. There is really no end to what you can print. If you do travel to conventions and have a booth, a professional banner will help attract people to your table. Someone once told me they were afraid to approach a table with one author selling one book. The author looked pretty desperate. He suggested indie authors should sit at one table together so the consumer has a choice of books to choose from.

Be careful with printing too many time limited promo items. I had printed several thousand promo cards to hand out at a convention in conjunction with a free limited time book release promo, but only gave out about half. In the end, I had to toss out a few thousand cards since they had time sensitive information. It was painful to throw out money, so spend wisely!

9. Press Releases and Press Kit

A press release is a written record you send to the news media about a topic that is newsworthy. There is no guarantee a media outlet will pick up your press release, but if anyone does, there is a good chance your book sales will increase exponentially.

A few press release sites include crowdfundingpr.org, pr.com, prfocus.com, pressreleaseping.com, pr-inside.com, newswire.com, prlog.org, 1888pressrelease.com, and free-press-release.com. When using these sites, you will have to open a free account before uploading your press release. Most of them have free options and all of them have packages you can buy to spread the release further than a few chosen news categories.

A press or media kit contains information about your book and is aimed at the media as well as potential readers. Many authors have it available for immediate download on their website as a PDF document for anyone interested in reading more about their work. The kit doesn't have to be fancy, but should look professional. You might want to include a flyer of your book with its blurb, an excerpt, review quotes, and a picture of the cover. A sample Q &A with you or a bio could reveal more information that a reading consumer craves. Include contact information and where people can buy your book.

Remember that you will be using press releases and press kits to pitch more than your book's description. If you want the media to notice, you have to give them something they believe will make a good, popular story.

10. Create a Book Trailer

Similar to movies, many books have video trailers these days. Usually, it's a video about the plot of a book told through different images and voiceovers. Some trailers with higher budgets have actors depicting scenes from the book.

If you can create a book cover, you can create a trailer. Video production software is available for free, such as Windows Movie Maker (windows.microsoft.com) or Apple iMovie (apple.com) for Mac. There are also paid ones, which are much more powerful. Of course you can always hire a freelancer from the same sites where you find artists and cover designers to help you create a trailer.

Before creating a book trailer, you will need to think

about what you want to present. Think about making a video as making a moving Power Point presentation with video or graphic footage combined with music and custom text. Write a script with scenes you think are captivating and then take some time to find images or video stock footage to match your vision. Keep the trailer to under two minutes as people don't have much patience to watch long videos. At the end of the video you will obviously have an image of your book and show them where to buy it.

I use Windows Movie Maker to make my book trailers because it came installed on my computer. Excellent free professional video stock footage can be obtained from sites such as stockfootageforfree.com, xstockvideo.com, archive.org and thecliparchive.com. For still images, royalty free graphics are available from pixabay.com, freeimages.com, or istockphoto.com. You can also create custom PowerPoint slides and save them as images for use in the video. If you want music, you can download some royalty free music from freemusicarchive.org. The program also has an option to add text with options of font size, color, and special animation effects. For a free tool, Movie Maker is great, but there are limitations, such as the inability to add links for people to click on to buy your book. A good forum to look for help is windowsmoviemakers.net where people post solutions to problems.

Most of your time will be spent looking for video footage and images that could work with your script for the book trailer. Unless you shoot your own custom footage, you may have to compromise your vision. Please remember to credit the resources at the end because it is the decent thing to do, since they are all free for use.

11. Book Competitions

There are many book competitions available in which

you can send a copy of your novel and enter to win a prize and some publicity for your book. Competitions are free or may charge a fee for entry. The chances of winning depends on the number of competing entries in your book's category. Regardless, for the rest of the book's life you can say it was nominated or entered into such and such a competition.

12. Book Giveaways or Draws

Goodreads is a popular forum for events and giveaways you can create. Book review sites often have draws for their readers. Basically, you can give out print or eBook copies of your book through platforms that already have a huge audience in place. They will help you advertise the giveaway or draw and you may gain some new readers in return.

13. Advertising: Radio, Television, Print, Internet

Professional radio, television, and print (magazines, newspapers) advertising will cost a pretty penny. There may be less costly, smaller media outlets available, just be sure the community is the right potential audience for your book. Prior to signing up for any advertising, make sure you be getting professional sounding and/or looking ads. This may involve hiring a graphic designer or voice actors. I purchased a radio ad with a smaller station and they were willing to throw in free voice work, which was awesome.

Another way of advertising is public speaking opportunities. Offering your time as a guest on a radio show or television show on a topic you specialize in. There are many online radio shows and local cable television shows searching for content all the time. Do a search online in relation to a subject you are confident speaking about and make contact. Having done both live and online radio shows, I have to say that they were fun. The host will let you know what they will ask so you can think of what you want to say before they record.

Internet advertising is relatively cheap compared to radio, television, and print because there are a lot more amateur options available. Doing a quick search on fiverr.com will yield many people willing to advertise on social media starting at $5. Social media tools like Facebook also offer internet ads you can tailor to be directed at certain audiences.

14. *Online Book Tours*

There are many book blog websites offering a chance for authors to promote their books. You can write to each website individually, or hire a freelancer or internet company that specifically helps you spread your message onto different sites. Specific messaging, like a cover reveal, interview with the author, and/or sale information over the book description and your social media connections is scheduled to be posted on a variety of other websites over a time period, sometimes several days in a row or maybe weekly over a month or more. Some packages have you write blog entries on a certain topic to let people learn about you and your work. All of these methods may lead to new readers for your book and new followers in your social network, positioning you to keep more and more people informed of your book promotions. Blog touring is the virtual version of a band playing on the road at different venues, except less exciting.

Generally, it takes a lot more time to organize a book tour yourself as you have to make connections specializing freelancers or companies will already have, prepare all the materials, and manage the schedule and activity of the event, sacrificing personal time or writing time. There is an incredible choice of paying services with costs ranging from $50-$2000 depending on the details and size of your tour.

15. *Cover and Book Trailer Reveals*

To build up excitement for your book, cover or book

trailer reveals can show off your work in an eye catching, exciting way. Just give little hints on social media about something happening on a specific date, then reveal your new book cover or trailer. The larger your existing audience is on internet channels (email sign ups on your website, social network followers and likes), the more potential buyers you will reach.

16. Book Reading or Book Launches

It is difficult to do book readings or book launches unless you already have an audience. The last thing you want is an empty room with a buffet table of food you've paid for. Generally, I don't recommend doing them on your own unless you can think of them as throwing a party for your friends and family to help get them excited about a book project you finished.

If you can partner up with another author or bookstore to split the costs, and advertise it well, it may be worth doing so to gain a new audience. Even if people don't come to see you specifically, they are there for another author and will discover you in the process.

17. Donate Your Book

Various places such as libraries, retirement homes, doctor's offices, and community centers may take book donations. This could be a costly venture and the audience is not targeted, but if you live in a small community you could become a local celebrity.

18. Guest Speaking: Libraries, Schools, Book Clubs, Book Stores, Conventions

Even if you offer your services for free, your time and travel accommodations cost something, so don't over offer yourself to speaking arrangements. One of my friends is an artist and his main venue for marketing and selling are comic conventions. Renting a table costs $100-$1200 depending on how big the convention is. He has to consider travel time, transportation, meals, and hotel rooms if a convention isn't local and decide if he feels the return will be worth the investment.

Authors have more choices because there are more venues available to market books, such as libraries, schools, book clubs, and book stores, in addition to various types of conventions like book fairs, trade shows, and expos with book award ceremonies. Look at what each venue is interested in. Do they want someone to talk about art? Talk about how you worked with an artist on the book cover. Do they want to learn about social media? Offer to share what you've learned about building an author platform. Generally, offer something more than just your book because if you can make the audience pay attention—they'll be curious about you to pick up your book.

These are only a few marketing ideas to get you started. Many of these things could be in place prior to your book's publishing date if you want to build sales momentum with a book launch promotion. After the book comes out, continuously do marketing if you want to maintain sales.

Publishing a book is like having a child that you have to take care of for the rest of its life. Adding more titles will help with the sales momentum as marketing efforts for each book will help sales overall. This is because once people discover one book, they may buy the rest of the author's titles as well. As a professor told me once, if you don't toot your own horn, no one will do it for you!

THE REALITY OF CROWD FUNDING

"Money often costs too much."

–Ralph Waldo Emerson

What is Crowdfunding?

Crowdfunding is a way of raising funds for a project or venture by collecting monetary donations from a large number of people, typically via the internet. According to Forbes magazine, crowdfunding websites helped raise $2.66 billion USD in 2012 and over $5.1 billion USD in 2013. In 2012, there were over one million individual campaigns for projects globally. Crowdfunding is not a charity as donors expect to receive something in return.

To raise money, a person or company promotes a project idea on a crowdfunding website who takes a cut of the funding as their commission. People who give money to the project are promised a reward for their contribution. There are two types of rewards: a product/service and equity, meaning backers receive shares in a company's future profits. For books, crowdfunding is similar to pre-selling your book to readers with special goodies that won't be available after the book reaches the market. A person giving money to the campaign is usually called a backer and not a donor as they are not donating to your cause but expect something in return.

For my first novel, *The Undead Sorceress*, I ran a Kickstarter crowdfunding campaign to raise money for book packaging and marketing services. I gave people a variety of incentives ranging from e-books, print books, bookmarks, posters, custom art to anime convention passes. Incentives for donations must be directly related to the book or something you create.

It took about 24 days to reach my $2500 USD goal. Two out of forty nine backers were strangers, which is only 4%. I have read that the typical Kickstarter campaign is funded 80% friends and family, with the remaining 20% being strangers. Strangers who are willing to support your project are genuinely interested and can tell you something about your target market, as well as be the beginning of a fan base if cultivated.

Professor Ethan Mollick of the Wharton School of the University of Pennsylvania contacted me recently to participate in his latest study on crowdfunding. In past studies, he concluded that crowdfunding democratizes access to funding, so groups at a disadvantage for gaining access to money are able to raise funds. As well, fraud is rare, though delays are common with over 75% of projects delivered late. You can read more about his research at http://crowdfunding.wharton.upenn.edu/research.

Crowdfunding Options

Stepping back, Kickstarter (kickstarter.com) is just one of many crowd funding websites available. At this time, there are about fifty sites one can choose from—easily found through search engines—but Kickstarter is the most popular. Indiegogo (indiegogo.com) was another crowd funding site I considered before Kickstarter opened its doors to Canadians in 2013. I decided to go with Kickstarter because it had more public interest. Indiegogo admittedly does have an advantage with their policy that if you do not reach your goal, you can still keep the money donated less a higher administration fee. Sites such as Pubslush (pubslush.com), was created to publish and crowdfund books exclusively. It is going through many changes since it was taken over by another company. However, as a crowdfunding platform it is not the most popular for projects. Kickstarter, like most other crowdfunding platforms, is all or nothing, putting pressure on you to keep promoting your campaign or else your efforts will be fruitless.

The reality is that crowd funding campaigns are a lot of work and careful planning will be needed to ensure that after covering fees (roughly 10% of the raised funds), taxes, creation of the product, and shipping and handling, the profit is enough for the project costs you initially sought. If your project goes viral, you will receive more funding, but remember you also have more promises to fulfill.

Being too successful could be detrimental. Once upon a time, there was a super successful Kickstarter campaign for a 3D printer. On a small scale, the creator could provide the 3D printer machines, but on a large scale when the campaign went viral, the creator couldn't find the parts to fulfill so many backers. People started showing up at his door and calling his cell phone at all hours, and he had a nervous breakdown. This is the worst case scenario of a successful campaign. Before you start, know your limits and recognize the risks if your campaign does go viral.

The Three Phases of a Crowdfunding Campaign

Running of a crowdfunding campaign can be divided into three parts: 1) beginning, 2) middle, and 3) end. You will need to promote extensively for all of these stages after you press the "go live" button. Let's be honest, friends and family are not necessarily interested in your project, so you will have to aim at the widest audience possible. While describing these phases, I will go over what happened to me during my Kickstarter campaign.

The Beginning of the Campaign

The start of a crowdfunding campaign is not the moment you launch the campaign, but rather the few months ahead of the actual launch date. There is a lot of legwork to be done and the campaign website needs a few weeks to go through an approval process before anything can happen.

Before you do anything, look up successful and unsuccessful campaigns in the publishing category. I noticed that successful campaigns all had strong visuals, a short video under 4 minutes, clearly written incentives, a good story, and lots of project updates. Failed campaigns did not have a good video or had no video, lack of a good story, and you could tell little effort was put into making the campaign page. Why should I give my hard earned money to someone who didn't appear to value it?

Take your time and set up everything you need for the campaign.

a. Register for an Account

No matter which website you decide to go with for crowd funding, you will need to open an account and link your bank account or another method of payment collection to it. You will discover there are usually discussion forums and tons of how to resources after you sign up, as these websites will receive part of your funding so your success is in their best interest too. Take the time to look through all that they offer and you'll usually find everything from how to develop a good story to how to make a good video.

b. Create a Draft Project Page

Creating a draft project page begins the process of organizing all the details of your campaign and the data for the many information fields you have to fill in when you submit your project. If you know what is required ahead of time, you can think about what important information you want to convey and how it looks on a draft page.

c. Think of a Good Story or Pitch

When you launch your campaign, it will be one of hundreds being launched on that day, and running alongside hundreds if not thousands of others each day it is live. Crowdfunding has become very popular, so everyone is competing for the same dollars. Similar to hospital foundations, why would a donor give to one hospital and not another? Is it because there is more prestige or visible community work that differentiates the successful hospital? Or perhaps they understand the work of one hospital better?

You have to think the same way. Why should people take the time to donate to your book campaign? *The Undead Sorceress* is a multicultural vampire book I wrote with the hope that it would inspire others to write more culturally diverse stories for the fantasy genre. My campaign was aimed at serious fantasy readers who are tired of reading about the same paranormal creatures and plotlines. By introducing a new take on vampire mythology, I hoped to start a new trend in supernatural stories.

Overall, make sure your story is something you believe in. People are very fast to see right through "phonies" and you do not want to be called out for that. Thinking of a good story and pitch does take time, but if you wrote a book, surely you did it for a reason! Try to remember what sparked your writing and got you passionate enough to slave for hours over the manuscript. This is your story, remember that you know it better than anyone else and you have to show what is special about it over and over again.

d. Think of Good Incentives

Book campaigns usually offer free books, bookmarks, posters, and t-shirts. Some campaigns even offered to create a custom character in their book, which is quite a lot of work and can create a major issue if the backer is not pleased with the written description of their character. Being creative in order to stand out in this area of the campaign is just as important as your efforts in the rest of it. Remember to consider all the costs, time and money, and limit the number of incentive levels to something manageable.

One incentive I offered was a custom portrait. To do this, I made a deal with some artists ahead of time to secure their services. Another one was convention passes for an anime convention where I volunteer. I contacted the organizers ahead of time as passes tend to sell out quickly. For both parties, I stipulated that the artwork or passes to the convention would not be required unless backers chose these options and only a limited number was made available. This meant that I did not have to pay anything ahead of time for items that may not be needed.

Research costs and outline a budget so you know what you can offer and effectively avoid a net negative campaign. Custom items will involve some work and you may have to cut deals with people in your network, which takes time. Make sure the deals are in place as you do not want to promise something you can't deliver.

e. Determine What the Project Goal Should Be

I have seen goals ranging from $800 USD to $30,000 USD. It is difficult to reach a high goal level for a book unless you already have a huge fan base or very rich friends. An author's reasoning for goal amounts should look at everything they plan to do for their book, from editing to marketing, and determine if they will crowdfund all or part of that plan. Let's be honest, the project goal may have to be less than the cost of the project in order to set a goal you think you can achieve. Other than book production and marketing, remember there are also costs related to fulfilling your incentives, taxes, and crowd funding website fees. Think of this entire campaign as a marketing exercise and a test to see if the market is willing to buy your book. If you have a really crappy idea, friends and family will probably turn the other way and pretend they didn't know you had a campaign running. Just pick a number you feel you can achieve and don't count on anything viral to happen because it probably won't. If it does, you are a very lucky person!

f. Make a Video

In a survey of 7,196 Kickstarter campaigns conducted by MWPDigitalMedia in 2013, they found that 56% of campaigns fail. If a video was made for the campaign, the chance of success increased by 85%. Their website blog (mwpdigitalmedia.com/blog) gives tips on how to make a good video.

While looking at other Kickstarter projects, I saw one campaign for a book sequel in which the video was particularly awful. Dressed in a suit and pretending to be a high power executive, the person acted super arrogant and rude. Why would I give my money to someone acting like a jerk? The book and story sounded great, but as soon as I saw this video, it was game over. One should act humble when asking for help. If you don't seem like you want the money, people will conclude you don't really need it, or deserve it. You should not act desperate, but speak with confidence and passion about your project. Keep the video under 4 minutes because interest will taper off if it is too long.

Writing a script for the video will take some time as you will most likely have to cut down on all the things you want to say. The expectations for videos are really high as I discovered after sending a draft video to some friends. They expected HD quality videos even though they knew I had no budget. After some research, I found websites offering free professional video stock footage, similar to free stock art. This was a life saver because they supplied video images, which were much more professional looking. You can make a book trailer from free software such as Windows Movie Maker or Apple iMovie for Mac as mentioned before in the marketing chapter. Free professional video stock footage can be obtained from sites such as stockfootageforfree.com, xstockvideo.com, archive.org, and thecliparchive.com. For royalty free graphic images, I visited pixabay.com, freeimages.com, and istockphoto.com. If you want music, you can download some royalty free music from freemusicarchive.org.

Don't be deterred thinking this may be a difficult task, because it is not. If you know how to use a word processor, you can use Movie Maker. Most of your time will be spent looking for video footages and images to work with your script. Unless you shoot your own custom footage, you will have to compromise your vision. Remember to credit the resources at the end because it is a decent thing to do, since they are all free for use.

g. Importance of Visuals

Crowdfunding campaigns need to be very visual because people may not read through anything that appears just wordy. Some may only look at the pictures on your page. If the visuals look crappy, they may decide not to donate.

If you don't have a budget for custom artwork, use interesting fonts and borders to divide up each section of the information on the campaign page. Using stock art may not always be a good idea if you don't want people to associate elements or characters from your book with those images.

A lot of successful campaigns and fantasy books on Kickstarter had lots of artwork, which is why I decided to splurge on concept art for my book. For a non-fiction book campaign, I would not have as much art and would rely on writing an interesting story that's short and sweet. If the story is too long, people will stop reading it because attention span is fleeting these days.

h. Pre-Promoting Campaign

You read this correctly. Before you press "go" on the launch button, you have to promote it. I had spoken to friends and family months ahead of time to let them know what I was doing. They were knocking on my door before the campaign started to make sure they didn't miss the funding window.

Post on social media, community forums, and any venue you can. Hopefully, you have lots of friends in your network who will become donors, giving a reason for strangers to have interest. Talk, tweet, post, write, and do whatever you need to do to spread the message that you are creating something exciting!

The Middle of the Campaign

The middle of the campaign starts the moment you press the "launch" button on the website. Admittedly, I was surprised by how stressful this part was. I thought I had done so much prep work in the beginning that I had nothing to worry about, but I was wrong!

After starting a campaign, you will have access to a dashboard where you keep track of all your supporters and funding amounts. You will spend a lot of time checking this dashboard and counting down how much you still need to reach your goal! Your campaign will pick up speed from your faithful friends and family members in the beginning, then start slowing down. Constant marketing work is required to attract future donors or to remind forgetful friends and family members you still need their help. Continuously working to gain more and more public exposure during the project will be very important to achieving success.

a. Write a Press Release

The point of a press release is to get media attention. Sometimes they don't go anywhere, but there is a small chance that a reporter somewhere may take interest in your campaign and it may go viral. A friend who was involved in a Kickstarter campaign featuring "half cats" was lucky enough to be the subject of a newspaper story and they raised almost 300% of what they asked for. They aimed for $5K USD and got over $14K USD. He encouraged me to send out as many PR releases as possible.

I wrote to many reporters by looking up contact information at different newspaper sites from Toronto Star to New York Times, but my campaign story was not compelling enough to catch their attention. However, some websites did pick up my press release, and to this day, when I do a search in regards to my Kickstarter campaign, I can still see my press releases floating around on the internet.

A few press release sites include crowdfundingpr.org, pr.com, prfocus.com, pressreleaseping.com, pr-inside.com, newswire.com, prlog.org, 1888pressrelease.com, and free-press-release.com. When using these sites, you will have to open a free account before uploading your press release.

Most of them have free options and all of them have packages you can buy to spread the release further.

b. Spend Time on Social Media

This is the time you can use your social media network to your advantage by posting updates and talking about your project. Don't do too much campaigning or people will become annoyed. Use Hootsuite to schedule messages to different social media accounts all at once for the entire campaign period.

c. Contact Sites and Forums Specializing in Crowdfunding

There are various crowd funding networks which help promote projects and you can post a message to let people know you have a live Kickstarter project. Sometimes the moderator of the group will send you various links and suggest you connect with other groups as well. Be aware that much of the audience on these networks may also be crowd funding, and don't expect them to fund yours. I've funded a few and never got funding back, so don't approach it as a reciprocal area of business, like sharing tweets on Twitter. Keep in mind you are one out of thousands of running projects in the same time frame.

Find these specialty groups by doing a search on whatever social media you are using and ask to join. Most of them have low barriers to entry and over time you can see which ones are more active than others. Some crowd funding interest sites such as crowdfundingforum.com have good forums to post questions and share frustrations. People will share ideas and suggestions you can use to improve campaign outcomes.

Other groups and forums should be specific to your book's genre to gain readers. Some feedback I got from the fantasy genre audience was that they would want to buy the book after its release, which made me realize they would rather invest in a sure thing. A crowdfunding campaign was too theoretical. They wanted to buy something already in existence rather than a book that may come out in the future. It was good experience to learn where some readers of my genre hung out, so I bookmarked these sites for later use.

Some sites and forums to visit include:

crowdcrux.com
crowdfundingpr.org
crowdfundingforum.com
reddit.com/r/kickstarter
fantasy-faction.com/forum.

Linked In and Google + also have many groups where you can discuss your campaign efforts.

d. Plan a Party

Since friends and family were going to be my main supporters, I planned a party and invited them to celebrate the project with them. During the party, people asked me to do a book reading. This was the first book reading I had ever done, and was even more memorable for being in front of friends and family. The party was worth it just for a happy memory I will always have from my first book and it felt good to reward my most loyal supporters.

e. Read About Successful Campaigns

There are many people who have made lots of money via crowd funding and you can find many interviews available online in which they are asked about their campaign secrets. These people worked hard and were lucky enough to get attention. It boils down to either having generous friends, online supporters, or good timing with the media. A very good site to visit for tips is www.crowdcrux.com. Continuing to look at how others have been successful can help you keep your efforts fresh and targeted during the campaign.

The End of the Campaign

When you reach the end of the campaign, regardless of whether it was a success or failure, you should send out thank you emails and take the opportunity to tell everyone your next steps. You will have learned a lot by the time the project ends and remember, this is a marketing exercise, even if it doesn't end up covering your financial goal.

If the campaign was a failure, thanking your supporters establishes a rapport so you can contact them again when your book actually comes out. Maybe you can offer these early supporters a bonus with their book purchase, such as an exclusive book mark or poster. Keep your early followers faithful by treating them well and they will be your strongest future advocates!

After reading all of this, you may not want to attempt a campaign. To be honest, if I had known how much work it was going to be, I'm not sure if I would have tried either. However, I learned a lot, and it pushed me out of my comfort zone by forcing me to learn many new things. No one else will sell your book for you and everything you can learn about funding and/or bringing attention to your book can only help you long term.

The art of how to sell without direct sell pitching is difficult to learn and my crowdfunding campaign helped me immensely. Rejection is a big part of marketing, so developing a thick skin will help as you build your indie author career!

AFTERWORD

One night after working late on my first book, I had a dream. An elephant on a space ship was shoveling piles of money into a machine. There were loud churning noises, then out came books plopping down one by one onto a conveyer belt. The elephant seemed pleased as he snatched one from the conveyor belt running into infinity, and he sat down calmly to read with a cup of tea. Elephants are very smart creatures with incredibly long memories and for some reason, the image of a reading elephant got stuck in my head.

– J F Garrard

I had been trying to come up with a book title other than *Self-Publishing 101* or *Introduction to Indie Publishing* and I hope my quirky title based in part on a reading elephant from my dream will convey a message that indie publishing is joyful, rewarding, and will hopefully bring in some extra cash. While money can't buy happiness, it can buy those expensive green tea mochi ice cream treats I crave. The elephant also seemed fitting because you need to know that the work load of publishing and marketing a book is enormous, like the elephant. Be prepared and take a breath after the work of writing to plan your next steps out, including all the skills you'll need to learn to be successful.

The appendix contains a basic budget sheet to help you think about finances, an example of how much I spent on my first book, and a list of links to resources mentioned throughout the book. Indie publishing is not rocket science and although frustrating at times, this will be one of the most rewarding things you ever do.

I keep thinking about leaving a legacy with books because quite a few people I know died in the year this book was released. I have a great fear of not finishing and publishing books already in my head. Creating art is what makes us human and a book is art with words.

Best of luck on your journey! Do get in touch and let me know about your books and I can post a link of your cover on my website and vice versa. Being an indie author is a long, hard road and you can never have too many friends!

APPENDICES

1. Basic Budget Sheet

Instructions:

1. Evaluate each column and identify what you can do yourself/find a friend versus hiring services
2. Remember that even if you choose DIY, you will still need tools such as software
3. Blank lines added in Marketing and Crowd funding section gives some extra room to expand that area as costs and planning vary person to person

Download the budget Sheet in Word or Excel format from:
http://www.darkhelixpress.com/non-fiction-books/literary-elephant/

Book Production Budget	DIY/Find a Friend ($)	Hiring Professionals ($)	Notes
Editing			
• In-Depth Editing			
• Copy Editing			
• Proofreading			
Cover Creation			
• Graphic Software			
• Stockart			
• Illustrated art			
• Cover Designer			
• Graphic Artist			
Formatting			
• Formatting Software			
• Formatter			
Distribution			
• Distribution Fees			
Business Items			
• Copyright Filing			
• ISBN			
• Incorporating			
Marketing			
•			
•			
•			
Inventory			
• Print Book Costs			
Crowd funding Campaign			
•			
TOTAL			

2. Sample Budget Sheet

This is a sample budget made for *The Undead Sorceress*, a 120K word count fantasy novel, which was a Kickstarter project. This was my first book, so I ended up spending way too much on it due to inexperience. I do not expect to break even until I write more books since this is a series. Maybe after book five, I might break even!

Publishing a book is a big financial commitment, so make sure your significant other supports you! The Kickstarter did bring in some funds, but not enough to cover the entire cost of the book. After learning so much from publishing this one book, the next book will cost less since all the connections have been made for competent professionals whom I can hire again and I know where I made mistakes in spending. Many authors don't go to conventions, so that is a huge cost you might not have.

Book Production Budget	DIY ($)	Hiring Professionals ($)	Notes
Editing			I already have Word, so I did not include the cost for it in this budget
• **Editor #1**	0		Husband did one round
• **Editor #2**	0		Friend did one round
• **Editor #3 (amateur from Fiverr) In-Depth Editing**		300	Terrible experience with amateur editor, tossed out all their work.
• **Editor #4 In-Depth Editing , Copy Editing**		1500	Professional editor recommended by a friend, fantastic job!
• **Editor #3 Proofreading**		200	Last minute panic attack, hired a proof reader for final check before printing.

Cover Creation			
• **Graphic Software**	0		Downloaded free paint.net program which can be found at getpaint.net
• **Stockart**	0		
• **Illustrated art**		500	Hired artist to create book cover illustration
• **Cover Designer**	0		Cover designer wouldn't work with me—my specs scared him—so I designed cover myself.
• **Graphic Artist**		200	Hired graphic artists to create a picture of myself to use on website, logo for vampire book series, and logo for Dark Helix Press publishing company.
Formatting			
• **Formatting Software**	50		Bought Scrivener to try. It's good for writing, but not so good for print formatting. I bought the Windows version, which has less options than the Mac version.
• **Formatter**		300	Found a great formatter based in Australia to format eBook and print book.
Distribution			
• **Distribution Fees**	0		Decided to just upload onto Amazon CreateSpace and Kindle Direct Publishing (KDP).
Business Items			
• **Copyright Filing**	100		

• ISBN	0		Canadians get free ISBNs.
• Incorporating		1500	Hired lawyer and accountant to help navigate the incorporation of a publishing company.
Marketing			
• Author website		150	Domain name registration, annual website maintenance fees ($100)
• Bookmarks		50	Printed book marks to promote book
• Limited time free book download promotional postcards		200	For distribution at an anime convention with attendance of 20,000
• Limited time free book download online advertising		100	Hired people to help spread message across social media
• Gave away free print books via Goodreads contest		100	Cost included books and postage
• Gave away eBooks via book review websites	0		Emailed PDF versions of the book to winners
• Book launches		300	Food & drinks for multiple book launches at different venues and jointly with other authors
• Banners & Table props		100	For book selling table at conventions
• Online radio ad and radio show		100	Travel expenses to do an online radio show and bought an ad to promote book

• **Travel expenses for speaking at conventions**		2000	Going to conventions is a hobby, but there are hotel & travel costs which add up when you visit a few in a year
Inventory			
• **Proof book costs**		200	Printed 10 proof copies, shipping was really expensive as I paid for rushed shipping
• **Print Book Costs**		2500	Printed 300 copies, which was too much. Will not do again. Ever. People can order when they want via POD so there was no need for me to stock up on so many copies.
Crowd funding Campaign			
• **Kickstarter campaign postcards**		50	
• **Concept Art**		500	Hired artist to create concept art for Kickstarter campaign
• **Incentives – t-shirts, posters, bookmarks, postcards, shipping print book costs**		300	Issue – a few backers didn't remember to kick in shipping costs, so I covered for them
TOTAL			**11,300**

3.   Summary of Resources

Below is a list of the websites mentioned throughout the book, which you can visit for more information about any particular topic.

Chapter 1 - The Different Paths of Publishing

Sites to research literary agents:

- agentquery.com
- querytracker.net
- writersmarket.com
- publishersmarketplace.com

Chapter 2 - Polishing the Manuscript

Where to Find Editors:

- The Editorial Freelancers Association (the-efa.org)
- Editors' Association of Canada (www.editors.ca)
- American Copy Editors Society (copydesk.org)
- Editorial Freelancers Association (copyediting.com)
- National Association of Independent Writers and Editors (naiwe.com).
- RedAdeptPublishing.com
- createspace.com
- reedsy.com
- fiverr.com
- upwork.com
- freelancer.com
- Bibliocrunch.com
- Authors Helping Authors Community (authorshelpingauthors.wordpress.com)

Chapter 3 - The Business of Selling Books

Copyright filing information:

- Canadian Intellectual Property Office (ic.gc.ca)
- The US Copyright office (copyright.gov)
- The UK Intellectual Property Office (gov.uk/government/organisations/intellectual-property-office)

Where to register or buy ISBNs:

- Library and Archives Canada (bac-lac.gc.ca)
- US RR Bowker (bowker.com)
- UK and Ireland Nielsen Book Services (isbn.nielsenbook.co.uk)

Where to create a free ISBN barcode:

- bookow.com

Cataloguing in publication information:

- Library and Archives Canada (bac-lac.gc.ca).
- US The Library of Congress (loc.gov)
- The British National Bibliography (bnb.bl.uk)

Chapter 4 - Distribution and Royalties

Royalty Calculators:

- Lulu: http://www.lulu.com/distribution/sell.php
- Createspace: createspace.com/Products/Book/Royalties.jsp
- Ingram Spark: ingramspark.com/Portal/Calculators/PubCompCalculator

Distribution, multi-channel sites:

- Smashwords (smashwords.com)
- Draft2Digital (draft2digital.com)

- Lulu (lulu.com)
- Amazon Kindle (kdp.amazon.com)
- Amazon CreateSpace (createspace.com)
- Amazon ACX (acx.com)
- Ingram Spark (ingramspark.com)

Distribution, single channel sites:

- Kobo (kobo.com/writinglife)
- Apple iBooks (apple.com/itunes/working-itunes/sell-content/books)
- Nook (www.nookpress.com/ebooks),
- Google Books (play.google.com/books/publish)
- Tolino (tolino-media.de)

Tax Consideration for Non-US Citizens, information for ITIN & EIN:

- IRS (irs.gov)

Chapter 5 - Formatting and Cover Creation

Formatting software:

- Calibre (calibre-ebook.com)
- iBooks Author (apple.com/ca/ibooks-author)
- Scrivener (literatureandlatte.com/scrivener.php)
- Jutoh (jutoh.com)
- Creatavist (creatavist.com)
- InDesign (adobe.com)

Cover Software:

- Paint.net (getpaint.net)
- Adobe Photoshop or Illustrator (adobe.com)

Royalty free graphics:

- pixabay.com
- freeimages.com

- istockphoto.com

Font sites:

- dafont.com
- fontsquirrel.com
- 1001freefonts.com
- fontmaster.com.

Where to create a free ISBN barcode:

- bookow.com

Where to search for a cover designer:

- bibliocrunch.com
- reedsy.com
- fiverr.com
- upwork.com
- freelancer.com
- 99designs.com

Where to search for an artist

- deviantart.com
- redbubble.com
- upwork.com
- fiverr.com
- freelancer.com
- 99designs.com.

Chapter 6 - The Marketing Black Hole

Create author profile pages:

- Amazon (authorcentral.amazon.com)
- Kobo (kobo.com/writinglife)
- Goodreads.com

Where to send Press Releases:

- pr.com
- prfocus.com
- prlog.org
- pr-inside.com
- newswire.com
- pressreleaseping.com
- 1888pressrelease.com
- free-press-release.com

Video production software:

- Windows Movie Maker (windows.microsoft.com)
- Apple iMovie (apple.com)

Royalty free video stock footage:

- stockfootageforfree.com
- xstockvideo.com
- archive.org.
- thecliparchive.com

Royalty free graphics:

- pixabay.com
- freeimages.com
- istockphoto.com

Royalty free music:

- freemusicarchive.org

Chapter 7 - The Reality of Crowd Funding

Video production software:

- Windows Movie Maker (windows.microsoft.com)
- Apple iMovie (apple.com)

Royalty free video stock footage:

- stockfootageforfree.com
- xstockvideo.com
- archive.org.
- thecliparchive.com

Royalty free graphics:

- pixabay.com
- freeimages.com
- istockphoto.com

Royalty free music:

- freemusicarchive.org

Where to send Press Releases:

- pr.com
- prfocus.com
- prlog.org
- pr-inside.com
- newswire.com
- pressreleaseping.com
- 1888pressrelease.com
- free-press-release.com

Sites and forums which have crowd funding discussions:

- crowdcrux.com
- crowdfundingpr.org
- crowdfundingforum.com
- reddit.com/r/kickstarter
- Linked In and Google +

Example of a forum specializing in fantasy genre:

- fantasy-faction.com/forum.

Read about successful campaigns:

- crowdcrux.com

Appendices

Budget Sheet download, Word or Excel format

- http://www.darkhelixpress.com/non-fiction-books/literary-elephant/

ABOUT THE AUTHOR

JF Garrard lives in Toronto, Canada. She is the President of Dark Helix Press, an Indie publisher of Multicultural Fantasy, Science Fiction and Raw Non-Fiction. She is interested in increasing awareness of diversity issues and breaking down cultural stereotypes through her dark stories. Her first novel, *The Undead Sorceress*, is a blend of Eastern and Western vampire mythologies. A germaphobe with a Nuclear Medicine background, you can find her speaking about writing and publishing at different Literature, Sci-Fi/Fantasy and Japanese Animation conventions throughout the year. www.jfgarrard.com

www.ingramcontent.com/pod-product-compliance
Lightning Source LLC
Chambersburg PA
CBHW021127020426
42331CB00005B/652